SOCIAL ISSUES, JUSTICE AND STATUS

THE FEDERAL EMPLOYEES' COMPENSATION ACT (FECA)

SOCIAL ISSUES, JUSTICE AND STATUS

Additional books in this series can be found on Nova's website under the Series tab.

Additional E-books in this series can be found on Nova's website under the E-book tab.

AMERICAN POLITICAL, ECONOMIC, AND SECURITY ISSUES

Additional books in this series can be found on Nova's website under the Series tab.

Additional E-books in this series can be found on Nova's website under the E-book tab.

SOCIAL ISSUES, JUSTICE AND STATUS

THE FEDERAL EMPLOYEES' COMPENSATION ACT (FECA)

ADDISON K. JAMES
AND
FILIP E. DAVIS
EDITORS

Nova Science Publishers, Inc.
New York

For permission to use material from this book please contact us:
Telephone 631-231-7269; Fax 631-231-8175
Web Site: http://www.novapublishers.com

Library of Congress Cataloging-in-Publication Data

ISBN: 978-1-62081-729-2

Published by Nova Science Publishers, Inc. † New York

CONTENTS

PREFACE

The Federal Employees' Compensation Act (FECA) is the workers' compensation program for federal employees. Like all workers' compensation programs, FECA pays disability, survivors, and medical benefits, without fault, to employees who are injured or become ill in the course of their federal employment and the survivors of employees killed on the job. The FECA program is administered by the Department of Labor (DOL) and the costs of benefits are paid by each employees' host agency. Employees of the U.S. Postal Service (USPS) currently comprise the largest group of FECA beneficiaries and are responsible for the largest share of FECA benefits. This book examines the key policy issues facing the FECA today, including the disproportionate share of claims and program costs attributed to postal workers, the payment of FECA benefits after retirement age, the overall generosity of FECA disability benefits as compared with those offered by the states, and the overall administration of the FECA program.

In: The Federal Employees' Compensation Act ISBN: 978-1-62081-729-2
Editors: A. K. James and F. E. Davis

Chapter 1

The Federal Employees' Compensation Act (FECA): Workers' Compensation for Federal Employees*

Scott Szymendera

Summary

The Federal Employees' Compensation Act (FECA) is the workers' compensation program for federal employees. Like all workers' compensation programs, FECA pays disability, survivors, and medical benefits, without fault, to employees who are injured or become ill in the course of their federal employment and the survivors of employees killed on the job. The FECA program is administered by the Department of Labor (DOL) and the costs of benefits are paid by each employee's host agency. Employees of the U.S. Postal Service (USPS) currently comprise the largest group of FECA beneficiaries and are responsible for the largest share of FECA benefits.

The modern FECA program can trace its roots to 1916 but has not been significantly amended since 1974. Today, the FECA program pays a basic disability benefit equal to two-thirds of an injured worker's pre-disability

* This is an edited, reformatted and augmented version of the Congressional Research Service Publication, CRS Report for Congress R42107, dated December 2, 2011.

wage, which rises to 75% of the pre-disability wage if the worker has any dependents. Benefits continue for the duration of disability or the life of the beneficiary and in cases of traumatic injuries, beneficiaries can receive a continuation of their full pay for the first 45 days. Persons with specific permanent partial disabilities, such as the loss of a limb, are entitled to disability benefits for a set number weeks provided by schedules set by statute and regulation. All medical costs associated with covered conditions are provided by the FECA program without any copayments, cost-sharing, or use of private insurance by the beneficiaries. The survivors of employees killed on the job are entitled to cash benefits based on the worker's wages and a modest benefit for funeral costs. Beneficiaries are also entitled to vocational rehabilitation services to assist them in returning to work.

In the 112th Congress, several committees have held hearings on the FECA program. These hearings have identified several key policy issues facing the program, including the disproportionate share of claims and program costs attributed to postal workers, the payment of FECA benefits after retirement age, the overall generosity of FECA disability benefits as compared with those offered by the states, and the administration of the FECA program.

To address some of these policy issues, committees in the House and Senate have ordered to be reported legislation that would make changes to the FECA program. In the House, H.R. 2309 would set financial conditions under which the USPS would be required to create a new workers' compensation system for its employees. Additional bills, H.R. 2465, passed by the House, and S. 1789, would make changes to the FECA program for all federal employees with the Senate legislation reducing benefit levels for beneficiaries over retirement age and eliminating augmented compensation for dependents.

Introduction

The Federal Employees' Compensation Act (FECA) is the workers' compensation system for federal employees. Every civilian employee of the federal government, including employees of the legislative and judicial branches, is covered by FECA, as are several other groups, including federal jurors and Peace Corps volunteers. In FY2009, the FECA program paid out more than $2.7 billion in benefits, including $1.8 billion in disability benefits, $847 million in medical benefits, and $138 million in benefits to the survivors of federal employees killed on the job.[1] In FY2009, administrative expenses made up 4.9% of total program costs.[2]

LEGISLATIVE HISTORY OF FECA

The FECA program has its origins in a law from the late 1800s that covered only the employees of a federal agency that has long since ceased to exist on its own. The modern FECA system has its roots in legislation enacted in 1916; many of the basic provisions of this original law, such as the basic rate of compensation, are still in effect today. Congress passed major amendments to the 1916 legislation in 1949, 1960, 1966, and most recently in 1974. Although these amendments made significant changes to the FECA program, the basic framework of the program endures as does the overall intent of Congress through the years to maintain a workers' compensation system for federal employees that is in line with the basic principles that have governed workers' compensation in this country for a century.

Limited Workers' Compensation for the United States Life Saving Service and Other Hazardous Federal Occupations

The first workers' compensation law for federal employees was enacted in 1882 and provided up to two years of salary to any member of the federal United States Life Saving Service disabled in the line of duty and two years of salary to his or her survivors in case of a line of duty death.[3] In 1908, Congress passed a more comprehensive workers' compensation law for federal employees engaged in certain hazardous occupations, such as laborers at federal manufacturing facilities and arsenals or workers at the construction of the Panama Canal. This law provided workers with up to one year of salary, after a 15-day waiting period, if disabled due to an employment-related injury and their survivors with up to a year of salary in case of death.

The 1882 and 1908 federal workers' compensation laws did not provide universal coverage for all federal employees. It is estimated that only one-fourth of the federal workforce was covered by the 1908 law, and the law was clearly designed only to provide coverage for what were seen to be the most hazardous jobs in the civil service.[4] President Theodore Roosevelt recognized this shortcoming of the law he would eventually sign. Before the 1908 law's passage, he called on Congress to pass a workers' compensation bill that would cover "all employees injured in the government service" and stated that the lack of such a comprehensive workers' compensation law was "a matter of humiliation to the nation."[5]

In addition to only covering a small portion of the federal workforce, the 1882 and 1908 laws did not provide for medical benefits for disabled workers, and the 1908 law only applied in cases of disability or death arising from injuries and not illnesses.

The Federal Employees' Compensation Act of 1916

President Woodrow Wilson signed the Federal Employees' Compensation Act, P.L. 64-267, into law on September 7, 1916, and in so doing extended the protections of the modern workers' compensation system to nearly all federal employees. This original FECA law remains the basis for the workers' compensation system for the federal civil service.

The FECA law provided coverage for nearly all civilian employees of the federal government injured or killed in line of duty. Coverage was not provided for occupational illnesses.[6] The law provided full medical coverage for covered injuries provided by government physicians and hospitals or private medical services selected by the government. Disability compensation was provided, after a three-day waiting period, at a rate of two-thirds of the worker's wage for total disability, with adjustments for partial disabilities. Disability benefits were subject to minimum and maximum levels specified in the law and neither benefits nor these levels were subject to any cost-of-living or other annual adjustments. The survivors of an employee killed on the job were entitled to cash benefits based on the worker's wage and were also entitled to a benefit to help offset funeral costs.

The 1916 legislation created the Federal Employees' Compensation Commission, with three members appointed by the President with the advice and consent of the Senate, to administer the FECA program. Benefit and administrative costs associated with the program were paid out of the Employees' Compensation Fund created by the law and financed with permanently authorized appropriations.

Congressional Intent

Bringing the Federal System in Line with the States

Congress had several clear intentions when drafting the FECA program in 1916. One such intention was to bring the protections offered to federal employees in line with those being offered by a majority of the states at the time, with the House Judiciary Committee reporting that such state laws were "working with most excellent results."[7] In addition, the committee reported that the schedule of compensation for disability in FECA was "in line with the best precedents found in State compensation acts," especially those in Massachusetts, New York, and Ohio.[8]

Providing Coverage to all Federal Employees

An additional intention of Congress was to provide workers' compensation coverage to all federal employees regardless of occupation, thus correcting what was seen as a shortcoming of the 1908 act. The House Judiciary Committee's report on the 1916 FECA legislation criticizes the limited coverage of the 1908 law and states,

> The present law, in denying compensation to an injured employee if his occupation was not "hazardous" goes counter to the theory on which all compensation acts are based, viz, that the industry shall bear the burden of injuries caused by it.[9]

This criticism of the limited coverage provided by the 1908 act, and the intention of the FECA legislation to correct this shortcoming, was echoed by the FECA legislation's sponsor in the Senate, Senator George Sutherland. Senator Sutherland, in a Senate Judiciary Committee hearing on the legislation, stated,

> The theory upon which compensation laws are drawn is that you are to compensate for the injury, not for the risk that the man ran in bringing about the injury; and under modern thought there is no logical reason for making distinction between what is hazardous and non-hazardous employment.[10]

Senator Sutherland reinforced his point with a rather graphic example stating "the clerk who has his leg cut off in his work about a store is just as effectively deprived of his leg as if it was cut off by a machine."[11]

Major FECA Amendments

Congress has passed major amendments to the FECA program in 1949, 1960, 1966, and most recently in 1974.

1949 Amendments

The Federal Employees' Compensation Act Amendments of 1949, P.L. 81-357, brought about the first set of significant changes to the FECA program since its inception in 1916. The 1949 amendments, in the words of the House Committee on Education and Labor, sought to "modernize and liberalize" the FECA program, which, according to the Senate Committee on Labor and Public Welfare, provided "only illusory security for most workers or their families."[12]

Increased FECA Coverage

The 1949 amendments expanded the scope of workers covered by the FECA program to include those classified as "officers" of the United States. The amendments also doubled the maximum disability benefit level, thus providing for a replacement of a larger portion of federal employee pay.

In addition to better meeting the goal of universal coverage of all employees, the inclusion of federal government officers was intended to provide FECA protections to previously excluded employees, such as Foreign Service Officers, who may serve in dangerous overseas areas. The increase in the maximum benefit level was necessary since, at the time, it was estimated by the Department of Labor (DOL) that 90% of FECA cases involved workers with wages that were essentially not covered by the program because of the low maximum benefit level.[13]

Increased FECA Benefits

Several provisions of the 1949 amendments effectively increased FECA benefits for workers and their survivors. The three-day waiting period for FECA disability compensation was eliminated in cases of disability lasting more than 21 days. A schedule of benefits for permanent partial disabilities was created for the first time, which permitted partial disability benefits to be paid without regard to actual impairment or wage loss. The elimination of the waiting period and creation of a benefits schedule were intended to bring the FECA program in line with state workers' compensation programs and the federal Longshore and Harbor Workers' Compensation Act program.[14]

The 1949 amendments provided for augmented compensation, in the amount of 8.33% of a workers' pre-disability wage, in cases in which an injured worker had at least one dependent. This augmented compensation, along with the standard compensation rate of two-thirds of the workers' wage, brought the level of FECA benefits for workers with dependents up to the current level of 75% of the worker's pre-disability wage. The benefit level for survivors was similarly increased. The intent of the augmented-compensation provision was to better insure that disabled workers and the survivors of workers killed on the job could provide economically for their dependents. The two-thirds benefit level for dependents was criticized by the House and Senate committees that reported the bill as "not sufficient as to ensure reasonable economic security to a family of a deceased worker where there is a large family."[15] Similar concerns over the adequacy of the two-thirds benefit level were expressed at a House Committee on Education and Labor hearing on the 1949 amendments.[16]

Reduced Benefits at Age 70

Although the 1949 amendments generally increased the level of FECA benefits, the amendments also required the FECA administrator to review the amount of compensation paid to any person aged 70 or older. The administrator was provided the authority to reduce the amount of such benefits if it was determined that the worker's wage-earning capacity had been reduced because of age, independent of his or her disability. This provision was opposed by several representatives from federal employee organizations who testified before the House Education and Labor Committee. They testified that such a provision was inconsistent with the mandatory federal employee retirement age of 70, in place at the time, and could cause undue hardships to workers who, because of their disabilities, had not been able to reach their full-earning potential or who had reduced pensions because of many years of limited or no earnings.[17]

Provisions for Vocational Rehabilitation

The 1949 amendments permitted the FECA program administrator to send beneficiaries to receive vocational rehabilitation services at the government's expense. The amendments also created a special supplemental benefit for workers participating in vocational rehabilitation programs. These provisions were intended to improve the return-to-work prospects of FECA claimants, which, it was thought, would ultimately benefit both the employee through a return to earning wages and the government through a reduction in FECA-benefit costs.[18]

The Exclusive Remedy Rule

The 1949 amendments established that the FECA program would be the exclusive remedy against the federal government for federal workers with employment-related injuries, illnesses, and deaths.

This provision prohibited employees from seeking to recover economic or non-economic damages from the government for injuries, illnesses, and deaths covered by FECA and brought the FECA program in line with one of the general principles of workers' compensation that was already written into the workers' compensation laws in the states.

When the FECA program was created, an exclusive remedy rule was seen as unnecessary because of the general prohibition against suits against the federal government.

However, by 1949, three factors had combined to result in significant numbers of federal employees choosing to bring lawsuits against the federal government rather than file for FECA benefits.

First, the passage after 1916 of laws, such as the Federal Tort Claims Act, which permitted some suits against the government.[19]

Second, some injuries to federal employees occurred while they worked for government corporations subject to lawsuits. Finally, because FECA benefits are limited by statute to partial wage replacement and medical benefits, employees felt that they could secure greater financial benefits from the courts than from the FECA program.[20]

1960 Amendments

The Chargeback Process

The Federal Employees' Compensation Act Amendments of 1960, P.L. 86-767, created the chargeback process in which the Secretary of Labor is required to bill each federal agency for the costs of FECA benefits provided to their employees in the previous fiscal year so that these agencies may reimburse the Employees' Compensation Fund. In addition, these amendments required that government corporations also pay their "fair share" of FECA administrative costs to the government. The chargeback process was intended by Congress to "further the promotion of safety" among federal agencies by making the agencies ultimately responsible for the costs of injuries, illnesses, and deaths of their employees.[21]

1966 Amendments

The Federal Employees' Compensation Act Amendments of 1966, P.L. 89-488, made two significant changes to the FECA program. These changes continue to be in effect today.

Use of the GS Scale to Set Minimum and Maximum Benefit Levels

Prior to the enactment of the 1966 amendments, the maximum and minimum levels of FECA benefits were set by statute and not subject to any automatic adjustments. In 1966, FECA benefits were still subject to levels enacted as part of the 1949 amendments. According to the Senate Committee on Labor and Public Welfare, the statutory maximum provided for full benefits for more than 99% of claimants in 1949, but only 85% of claimants by 1966.[22] To address the difficulty inherent in using statutory changes to keep pace with the growth in federal employees' wages, the 1966 amendments provide for use of the general schedule (GS) scale as the basis for the maximum and minimum FECA benefit levels with the maximum level set at 75% of the highest rate of basic pay at the GS-15 level and the minimum level set at 75% of the lowest rate of basic pay at the GS-2 level.

Cost-of-Living Adjustment for Benefits

The 1966 amendments provided for an annual cost-of-living adjustment for FECA benefits.[23] This annual adjustment is a unique feature of the FECA program not found in other workers' compensation systems.

1974 Amendments

The Federal Employees' Compensation Act Amendments of 1974, P.L. 93-416, made three major changes to the FECA program. These three changes remain key elements of the program today.

Continuation of Pay

The 1974 amendments provided for up to 45 days of continuation of pay from a worker's employing agency in cases of traumatic injuries covered by FECA. During this period, an injured employee may receive his or her full pay rather than FECA compensation. Because continuation of pay is considered income rather than a benefit, it is subject to the federal income tax and is reduced by all standard payroll deductions.

Congress felt that 45 days of continuation of pay were needed because of the time it often took for FECA claims to be processed and compensation benefits to begin. In its report on the 1974 amendments, the Senate Committee on Labor and Public Welfare cited a General Accounting Office report that stated that the average processing time for FECA claims was between 49 and 70 days, a delay that the committee found "creates economic hardship on the injured employee and his or her family and causes difficult administrative problems for the Secretary of Labor and the employing agencies."[24]

Employee Choice of Physician

The 1974 amendments authorized employees to select their own treating physicians rather than use doctors employed or selected by the federal government. The right of employees to have free choice over who provides their medical care was one of the recommendations of the National Commission on State Workmen's Compensation Laws in 1972; this provision brought the FECA program in line with that recommendation as well as some other workers' compensation systems.

Elimination of Reduced Benefits after Age 70

The 1974 amendments removed the provision, enacted as part of the 1949 amendments, requiring that FECA benefits be reviewed and permitting FECA benefits to be reduced after a claimant reached the age of 70 to account for the reduced earning capacity that may come with age independent of any disability. In its report on the 1974 amendments, the Senate Committee on Labor and Public Welfare provided the following justification for eliminating the reduced benefit provision:

> The Committee finds that such a review places an unnecessary burden on both the employees receiving compensation and the Secretary. Further, the fact that an employee reaches 70 has no bearing on his or her entitlement to benefits and is considered discriminatory in the Committee's opinion.[25]

Recent FECA Amendments

There have been no major amendments to the FECA program since 1974. However, the 109th and 110th Congresses did make changes to FECA that partially address two of the issues currently facing the program.

Change to the FECA Waiting Period for Postal Employees

Section 901 of the Postal Accountability and Enhancement Act, P.L. 109-435, changed the way the FECA three-day waiting period for compensation is applied to employees of the U.S. Postal Service (USPS). This provision requires that postal employees satisfy the three-day waiting period before the continuation of pay period can begin. All other federal employees continue to serve the three-day waiting period after the conclusion of the continuation of pay period and before FECA compensation benefits begin.

This provision was based on a recommendation of the President's Commission on the USPS. The commission's recommendation was part of a larger package of FECA reforms for postal employees intended to reduce the Postal Service's workers' compensation costs. Because of what the commission termed the "unique businesslike charter" of the Postal Service, the commission recommended that the service's workers' compensation system become more in line with the state workers' compensation systems that provide coverage for most private-sector businesses.[26]

Death Gratuity for Federal Employees Killed While Serving Alongside the Armed Forces

American military operations in Iraq and Afghanistan have been supported by an unprecedented number of civilian employees, some of whom are serving in hostile areas alongside the Armed Forces. These deployed civilian employees are covered by FECA, but concerns have been raised about the adequacy of FECA benefits for those injured or killed while serving in areas of combat, especially when compared with the benefits available to members of the Armed Forces from the Departments of Defense and Veterans Affairs.[27]

Section 1105 of the National Defense Authorization Act for Fiscal Year 2008, P.L. 110-181, provides for a death gratuity of up to $100,000 to be paid to the survivors of any federal employee, or employee of a non-appropriated fund instrumentality, who "dies of injuries incurred in connection with the employee's service with an Armed Force in a contingency operation." This death gratuity is paid in addition to the regular FECA compensation for survivors, but is offset by any other death gratuities paid by the federal government.

OVERVIEW OF THE FECA PROGRAM TODAY

Statutory and Regulatory Authorities

The FECA program is authorized in statute at 5 U.S.C. Sections 8101 *et seq*. Regulations implementing the FECA are provided at 20 C.F.R. Sections 10.00-10.826. The FECA program is administered by the Department of Labor, Office of Workers' Compensation Programs (OWCP).

Program Financing

Benefits under FECA are paid out of the federal Employees' Compensation Fund. This fund is financed by appropriations from Congress that are used to pay current FECA benefits and that are ultimately reimbursed by federal agencies through the chargeback process.

Each quarter OWCP provides to all federal agencies with employees receiving FECA benefits an estimate of the cost of these benefits to assist these agencies in preparing their budget requests. By August 15 of each year, OWCP sends each agency a statement of their FECA costs for the previous fiscal year. Each agency must include in its next budget request an appropriation to cover its FECA costs for the previous fiscal year. Upon receiving this appropriation, or if a non-appropriated entity of the government, by October 15, the agency must reimburse the Employees' Compensation Fund for the costs of the FECA benefits provided to its employees.

The administrative costs associated with the FECA program are provided to the DOL through the appropriations process. In addition, the USPS and certain other non-appropriated entities of the federal government are required to pay for the "fair share" of the costs of administering benefits for their employees. In 2010, the USPS paid approximately $61 million in FECA administrative costs.[28]

FECA Benefit and Administrative Costs

Table 1 provides data on the costs of providing FECA compensation and medical benefits as well as administrative costs associated with the FECA program. In FY2009, compensation benefits made up 68.7% of the nearly $2.8 billion in total FECA benefits and direct administrative costs made up 5.0% of total program costs.[29]

Employees Covered by FECA

The FECA program covers all civilians employed by the federal government, including employees in the executive, legislative, and judicial branches of the government. Both full-time and part-time workers are covered, as are most volunteers and all persons serving on federal juries. Coverage is also extended to certain groups, including state and local law enforcement officers acting in a federal capacity, federal jurors, Peace Corps volunteers, students participating in Reserve Officer Training Corps programs, and members of the Coast Guard Auxiliary and Civil Air Patrol.

Table 1. FECA Benefits and Costs, FY2009

	Cost in Thousands of Dollars	Percentage of Total Benefit/Program Costs
Compensation Benefits	1,900,156	68.7
Medical Benefits	863,729	31.3
Total Benefit Costs	*2,763,885*	*100.0*
Direct Administration	146,015	5.0
Total Program Costs	*2,909,900*	*100.0*

Source: Ishita Sengupta, Virginia Reno, and John F. Burton, Jr., *Workers' Compensation: Benefits, Coverage, and Costs, 2009*, National Academy of Social Insurance, Washington, DC, August 2011, p. 79.

Notes: Direct administrative costs are for the administration of FECA program by DOL's OWCP. Indirect administrative costs are for activities, such as investigations or legal support, outside of OWCP.

Conditions Covered by FECA

Under FECA, workers' compensation benefits are paid to any covered employee for any disability or death caused by any injury or illness sustained during the employee's work for the federal government. There is no list of covered conditions nor is there a list of conditions that are not covered. However, no injury, illness, or death may be compensated by FECA if the condition was

- caused by the willful misconduct of the employee;
- caused by the employee's intention to bring about the injury or death of himselfor another person; or
- proximately caused by the intoxication of the employee.

In addition, any person convicted of a felony related to the fraudulent application for or receipt of FECA benefits forfeits his or her rights to all FECA benefits for any injury that occurred on or before the date of conviction. The benefits of any person confined in jail, prison, or an institution pursuant to a felony conviction are suspended for the duration of the incarceration and may not be recovered.

FECA Claims Process

All FECA claims are processed and adjudicated by OWCP. Initial decisions on claims are made by OWCP staff based on evidence submitted by the claimant and his or her treating physician. The law also permits OWCP to order a claimant or beneficiary to submit to a medical examination from a doctor contracted to the federal government. An employee dissatisfied with a claims decision may request a hearing before OWCP or an OWCP review of the record of its decision. A final appeal can be made to the Employees' Compensation Appeals Board (ECAB). The decision of the ECAB is final, cannot be appealed, and is not subject to judicial review.

Time Limit for Filing FECA Claims

In general, a claim for disability or death benefits under FECA must be made within three years of the date of the injury or death. In the case of a latent disability, such as a condition caused by exposure to a toxic substance over time, the three-year time limit does not begin until the employee is disabled and is aware, or reasonably should be aware, that the disability was caused by his or her employment.

FECA Compensation Benefits

Continuation of Pay

In the case of a traumatic injury, an employee is eligible for continuation of pay.[30] Continuation of pay is paid by the employing agency and is equal to 100% of the employee's rate of pay at the time of the traumatic injury. Since continuation of pay is considered salary and not compensation, it is taxed and subject to any deductions normally made against the employee's salary. Any lost work time beyond 45 days, or lost time due to a latent condition, is considered either a partial or total disability under FECA.

Employees of the United States Postal Service must satisfy a three-day waiting period before becoming eligible for continuation of pay.

Partial Disability

If an employee is unable to work full-time at his or her previous job, but is able to work either part-time or at a job in a lower pay category, then he or she is considered partially disabled and eligible for the following compensation benefits:

- if the employee is single, a monthly benefit equal to two-thirds of the difference between the employee's pre-disability and post-disability monthly wage; or
- if the employee has at least one dependent, a monthly benefit equal to 75% of the difference between the employee's pre-disability and post-disability monthly wage.

The compensation benefits paid for partial disability are capped at 75% of the maximum basic pay at rate GS-15 (GS-15, step 10), are not subject to federal taxation, and are subject to an annual cost-of-living adjustment. Benefits are paid for the duration of the disability or the life of the beneficiary.

If an employee's actual wages do not accurately represent his or her true wage-earning capacity, or if he or she has no wages, then his or her partial disability benefit is based on his or her wage-earning capacity as determined by OWCP using a combination of vocational factors and "degree of physical impairment."

Scheduled Benefits

In cases in which an employee suffers a permanent partial disability, such as the loss of a limb, he or she is entitled to a scheduled benefit. The scheduled benefit is in addition to any other partial or total disability benefits received. An employee may receive a scheduled award even if he or she has returned to full-time work.[31] The list of scheduled benefits is provided in the **Appendix** to this report. If an employee suffers a disfigurement of the face, head, or neck that is of such severity that it may limit his or her ability to secure or retain employment, the employee is entitled to up to $3,500 in additional compensation.

Total Disability

If an employee is unable to work at all, then he or she is considered totally disabled and eligible for the following compensation benefits:

- if the employee is single, a monthly benefit equal to two-thirds of the employee's pre-disability monthly wage; or
- if the employee has at least one dependent, a monthly benefit equal to 75% of the employee's pre-disability monthly wage.

The compensation benefits paid for total disability are capped at 75% of the maximum basic pay at rate GS-15 (GS-15, step 10), are not subject to federal taxation, and are subject to an annual cost-of-living adjustment. Benefits are payable until it is determined that the employee is no longer totally disabled and may continue until the employee's death.

Death

If an employee dies on the job or from a latent condition caused by his or her employment, the employee's survivors are eligible for the following compensation benefits:

- if the employee's spouse has no children, then the spouse is eligible for a monthly benefit equal to 50% of the employee's monthly wage at the time of death; or
- if the employee's spouse has one or more children, then the spouse is eligible for a monthly benefit equal to 45% of the employee's monthly wage at the time of death and each child is eligible for a monthly benefit equal to 15% of the employee's monthly wage at the time of death, up to a maximum family benefit of 75% of the employee's monthly wage at the time of death.

Special rules apply in cases in which an employee dies without a spouse or children or with only children.

If a spouse remarries before the age of 55, then he or she is entitled to a lump-sum payment equal to 24 months of benefits, after which all benefits cease. If a spouse remarries at the age of 55 or older, benefits continue for life. A child's benefits end at the age of 18, or age 23 if the child is still in school. A child's benefits continue for life if the child is disabled and incapable of self-support.

The compensation benefits paid for death are capped at 75% of the maximum basic pay at rate GS-15, are not subject to federal taxation, and are subject to an annual cost-of-living adjustment.

Additional Death Benefits

The personal representative of the deceased employee is entitled to reimbursement, up to $200, of any costs associated with terminating the deceased employee's formal relationship with the federal government. The personal representative of the deceased employee is also entitled to a reimbursement of funeral costs up to $800, and the federal government will pay any costs associated with shipping a body from the place of death to the employee's home. An employee killed while working with the military in a contingency operation is also entitled to a special gratuity payment of up to $100,000 payable to his or her designated survivors.

FECA Medical Benefits

Under FECA, all medical costs—including medical devices, therapies, and medications— associated with the treatment of a covered injury or illness are paid for, in full, by the federal government. A FECA beneficiary is not responsible for any coinsurance or any other costs associated with his or her medical treatment and does not have to use any personal insurance for any covered medical costs. A published fee schedule is used by OWCP to determine the rate or reimbursement paid to medical providers.[32]

Generally, a beneficiary may select his or her own medical provider and is reimbursed for the costs associated with transportation to receive medical services. Medical providers must be authorized by OWCP and can have their authorization removed if it is determined that they are violating program rules or are involved in fraud.

A FECA beneficiary who is blind, paralyzed, or otherwise disabled such that he or she needs constant personal attendant care may receive an additional benefit of up to $1,500 per month.

Vocational Rehabilitation

The Secretary of Labor may direct any FECA beneficiary to participate in vocational rehabilitation, the costs of which are paid by the federal government. While participating in vocational rehabilitation, the beneficiary may receive an additional benefit of up to $200 per month. However, any beneficiary who is directed to participate in vocational rehabilitation and fails to do so may have his or her benefit reduced to a level consistent with the increased wage earning capacity that likely would have resulted from participation in vocational rehabilitation.

Coordination with Other Benefits

Coordination with Retirement Benefits for Federal Employees

Most federal employees are covered by either the Civil Service Retirement System (CSRS) or the Federal Employees' Retirement System (FERS).[33] The CSRS covers federal employees initially hired before January 1, 1984. The FERS covers employees hired after that date and CSRS-eligible employees who voluntarily switched to FERS coverage during "open seasons" held in 1986 and 1987. Employees contribute to the cost of the CSRS and FERS through payroll taxes.

Both the CSRS and FERS provide for defined benefit pensions for retired and disabled federal employees. The FERS defined benefit pension is smaller than that provided by the CSRS, however, the FERS also provides for participation in the Social Security system and the Thrift Savings Plan (TSP), a federally managed defined contribution plan similar to a 401(k) plan offered to private-sector workers.[34] While an injured federal employee is receiving FECA benefits and not working, he or she does not make any CSRS or FERS contributions, but does continue to accrue time in service for the purposes of retirement eligibility.[35] Because FECA benefits are not considered earnings under either the Social Security Act or Internal Revenue Code, FECA beneficiaries generally may not contribute to the Social Security system via the payroll tax or to the TSP.

Once a FECA beneficiary becomes eligible for CSRS or FERS retirement benefits, he or she may elect to receive these retirement benefits or remain in the FECA program for the duration of disability. Once this election is made, it may be changed at any time.

That amount of the FERS basic annuity is increased from 1% of the employee's high-three average pay to 2% of the high-three average pay for any period during which the employee was receiving FECA benefits rather than earnings.

This provision, enacted in 2003, is designed to partially replace retirement income lost because of the employee's inability to contribute to the Social Security system or the TSP while receiving FECA benefits.[36]

Coordination with Disability Retirement Benefits

Both the CSRS and FERS offer federal employees who are unable to continue working because of disabilities the option to take a disability retirement annuity before reaching normal retirement age.[37] For the purposes of the CSRS and FERS disability retirement systems, an employee is considered disabled and eligible for an annuity if he or she is unable to perform his or her current federal job and cannot be accommodated with a job at the same rate of pay by his or her employing-agency because of a medical condition that is expected to last at least one year. An employee must have five years of service to qualify for disability retirement benefits under CSRS and 18 month of service under FERS. Generally, the amount of an employee's disability annuity is lower than what the employee would have received had he or she worked until normal retirement age and collected a CSRS or FERS retirement annuity. As in the cases of a FERS or CSRS retirement annuity, a FECA beneficiary that is also eligible for CSRS or FERS disability retirement benefits may elect to receive these disability retirement benefits or remain in the FECA program for the duration of disability. Once this election is made, it may be changed at any time.

Coordination with Social Security Disability Insurance Benefits

Because FECA is a workers' compensation program, it is covered by the public disability offset provisions of Section 224 of the Social Security Act.[38] If a FECA beneficiary is also receiving Social Security Disability Insurance (SSDI) benefits, then the total amount of the beneficiary's monthly SSDI benefit, all SSDI benefits paid to his or her spouse or dependents, and his or her FECA benefit can not exceed 80% of his or her average monthly wage at the time of his or her disability.[39] The FECA beneficiary's SSDI benefits, or the benefits for his or her spouse or dependents, are reduced until the 80% threshold is reached.

Coordination with Social Security Retirement Benefits

Federal employees covered by the FERS system are also covered by the Social Security system for their periods of federal employment. If a federal employee covered by FERS is entitled to both FECA and Social Security retirement benefits, the amount of his or her monthly FECA benefit is reduced by the amount of his or her Social Security retirement benefit attributable to his or her federal service.

Selected Current Issues Facing the FECA Program

In the 112th Congress, the House and Senate have held hearings that have addressed several issues facing the FECA program, including the cost of FECA benefits for postal workers, the proper role of FECA compensation benefits for injured workers as they age, and comparisons between the FECA program and state workers' compensation programs that cover the majority of private-sector and state and local government workers in the country.[40]

FECA Legislation Ordered to be Reported in the 112th Congress

- Postal Reform Act of 2001, H.R. 2309
- 21st Century Postal Act of 2011, S. 1789

FECA Legislation Passed by the House of Representatives in the 112th Congress

- Federal Workers' Compensation Modernization and Improvement Act, H.R. 2465

In addition, as part of larger U.S. Postal Service (USPS) reform legislation, the House Committee on Oversight and Government Reform has ordered to be reported legislation (H.R. 2309) that would make changes to the FECA program as it applies to postal workers. The Senate Committee on Homeland Security and Governmental Affairs has ordered to be reported legislation (S. 1789) that would make significant reforms to the FECA program for all federal employees. The main vehicle for FECA program reform in the House is H.R. 2465, which was passed by the House and which would make changes to the FECA program for all federal employees.

FECA and the U.S. Postal Service

The USPS and its employees make up the largest component of the FECA program, and postal workers are injured on the job at rates disproportionate to the rest of the federal government. As shown in **Table 2**, although postal workers make up 21.2% of the federal workforce, they are responsible for

37.4% of injuries, illnesses, and fatalities that resulted in FECA cases in FY2010.[41]

The most significant area in which the experience of the USPS with the FECA program differs from that of the rest of the government is in the severity and duration of injuries and illnesses that result in FECA cases. As shown in **Table 3**, in FY2010, injuries and illnesses to postal workers resulted in 218.7 lost production days per 100 employees, compared with 77.4 days for the entire federal government and 34.8 days for non-postal federal entities.[42] This means that for every one of the nearly 600,000 postal workers, more than two days of work were lost due to injuries, illnesses, or fatalities and that an estimated total of 1,298,750 production days, or 4,995 work years at the USPS were lost in FY2010 due to injuries, illnesses, and fatalities.[43]

The USPS was the only federal entity with more than 200 lost production days per 100 employees in FY2010, and in FY2010 the only two other entities that had at least 150 lost production days were the Armed Forces Retirement Home and the International Boundary and Water Commission, small entities with approximately 250 employees each. The USPS in FY2010 was responsible for 60% of the total number of lost production days by the entire federal government.

Table 2. FECA Cases, FY2010

Category	Employees[a]		FECA Cases[b]		
	Total	Percentage	Total	Percentage	Per 100 Employees
Federal Government	2,804,206	100.0	108,587	100.0	3.9
U.S. Postal Service	593,850	21.2	40,588	37.4	6.8
Federal Government, excluding U.S. Postal Service	2,210,356	78.8	67,996	62.6	3.1

Source: Congressional Research Service (CRS) table with data taken from Department of Labor, Occupational Safety and Health Administration, *Federal Injury and Illness Statistics for Fiscal Year 2010*, http://www.osha.gov/dep/ fap/statistics/ fedprgms_stats10_final.html#footnote4a.

Note: Numbers may not add due to rounding and the number of federal employees calculated at different times during the year.

a. As of June 2010.

b. Includes all new injury, illness, and fatality cases submitted to FECA, less any denied claims.

Table 3. Lost Time FECA Cases and Lost Production Days due to Injuries, Illnesses, and Deaths, FY2010

	Lost Time Cases			Lost Production Days Per 100 Employees
Category	Total	Percentage	Per 100 Employees	
Federal Government	47,226	100.0	1.68	77.4
U.S. Postal Service	15,311	32.4	2.58	218.7
Federal Government, excluding U.S. Postal Service	31,915	67.6	1.44	34.8

Source: The Congressional Research Service (CRS) with data taken from Department of Labor, Occupational Safety and Health Administration, Federal Injury and Illness Statistics for Fiscal Year 2010, http://www.osha.gov/dep/fap/statistics/fedprgms_stats10_final.html#footnote4a; and Department of Labor, Office of Workers' Compensation Programs, FY2010 End of Year LPD Report for All Government, http://www.dol.gov/owcp/dfec/share/lpd/FY20104thQtr/All Government.htm.

Note: Numbers may not add due to rounding and the number of federal employees calculated at different times during the year.

Given the disproportionate number of injuries and lost production days attributed to the USPS, it is not surprising that benefits for postal workers make up a disproportionate share of the total costs of the FECA program. In chargeback year 2009, the FECA program paid approximately $2.7 billion in total benefits, with nearly $1.1 billion in benefits, or 40% of total benefits, being paid for claims by postal workers.[44]

As discussed earlier in this report, in 2006, with the enactment of P.L. 109-435, Congress changed the application of the three-day waiting period for postal workers with traumatic injuries with the goal of reducing FECA costs to the USPS. Under this provision, postal workers now must satisfy the three-day FECA waiting period before the beginning of the continuation of pay period, rather than after this period and before receiving FECA compensation.

Legislative Activity

The House postal reform legislation is the only one of the three active bills to directly address the FECA program for postal workers. Specifically, H.R. 2309 would require the U.S. Postal Service to design and implement a new workers' compensation system for its employees that would prohibit the payment of augmented compensation for dependents and require some form of transition to or coordination with retirement benefits. This requirement would only go into effect, however, if the Postal Service Financial Responsibility and Management Assistance Authority created by the legislation determines that the financial condition of the USPS warrants such a change.

FECA and Retirement Age

Both FECA compensation and medical benefits are payable for the duration of a person's disability. There is no maximum duration of benefits and no maximum age at which benefits must be terminated. Beneficiaries who are eligible for CSRS or FERS retirement or disability annuities may chose to remain in the FECA program. Given the level of benefits, which can be as high as 75% of a worker's pre-disability wage; the annual cost-of-living adjustment to benefits; and the fact that FECA benefits are not taxed, in some cases the monthly FECA benefit is higher than what would be paid by a CSRS or FERS annuity. In addition, because FECA beneficiaries who are not working do not pay into either the Social Security system or the TSP, they may be unable to rely on these programs as a significant source of retirement income.

The Department of Labor reports that although less than 2% of new injury cases stay on the FECA rolls for more than two years, approximately 45,000 cases currently receive long-term disability benefits and 15,000, or one-third of these cases involve beneficiaries aged 66 or older.[45] The U.S. Postal Service Office of Inspector General reports that the FECA rolls include 9,554 postal workers aged 55 or older; 3,389 aged 65 or older; and 928 aged 80 or older, including one aged 99.[46]

The provision of FECA compensation benefits to workers after retirement age has changed during the history of the FECA program. Although FECA benefits have always been paid for the duration of disability, between 1949 and 1974, the administrator of the FECA program was required to review the amount of benefits paid to each beneficiary at the age of 70 and was authorized to reduce the amount of such benefits if it was determined that the beneficiary's wage-earning capacity had been reduced by his or her age, independent of his or her disability.

This provision was repealed in 1974 with the Senate Committee on Labor and Public Welfare calling the reduction of benefits at the age of 70 "discriminatory."[47]

Policy Considerations

The question of whether FECA benefits should continue past retirement age depends somewhat on the intent of these benefits. If FECA disability benefits are intended solely to replace income lost by a worker because of an injury or illness, then one can reasonably argue that these benefits should stop at retirement age, when the worker would likely voluntarily stop working on his or her own, and thus no longer have wages to be replaced. It could be argued that the provision of FECA benefits for wage loss is analogous to the SSDI program, which stops paying benefits when a disabled beneficiary reaches retirement age. However, SSDI benefits automatically convert to Social Security retirement benefits at retirement age.

However, if FECA disability benefits are intended to provide some relief to the worker beyond wage replacement, such as providing additional money that might have been paid by an at-fault employer through the tort system or guaranteeing a certain minimum standard of living for a disabled worker, then stopping benefits at any age while the disability continues would violate this intent and deprive the beneficiary of deserved benefits.

Currently, 14 states and the District of Columbia place limitations on the duration of permanent total disability benefits under their workers' compensation systems. These limitations are in the form of a maximum number of weeks benefits may be paid, a termination of benefits at retirement or some other age, or a combination of both.[48] Federal workers' compensation benefits paid through the Longshore and Harbor Workers' Compensation Act are paid for the duration of disability or the life of the beneficiary.

Legislative Activity

The legislation in the Senate includes provisions that would limit benefits to persons over the retirement age. Specifically, S. 1789 would reduce the amount of the basic FECA disability benefit to 50% of a workers' pre-disability wage when he or she reaches the full-retirement age for Social Security.[49] Certain current beneficiaries with permanent total disabilities would not be affected by this provision.

In the House, FECA reform legislation (H.R. 2465) does not include any provisions that would change FECA benefit amounts for beneficiaries at retirement age. However, in July 2011, the chairman and ranking Member of the House Education and Workforce Committee and the Subcommittee on Workforce Protections wrote a letter to the comptroller general requesting that the Government Accountability Office (GAO) examine several policy proposals regarding the FECA program, including a proposal to reduce the

FECA benefits of persons over the Social Security full-retirement age to 50% of the pre-disability wage.[50]

FECA Benefit Generosity

In general, FECA disability benefits are more generous than those offered by state workers' compensation systems. For workers with traumatic injuries, FECA offers continuation of pay, at full salary, for the first 45 days. No state system currently provides any type of continuation of pay, absent the use of some form of sick or personal leave. Disability benefits under FECA are adjusted annually to reflect changes in the cost of living, a provision generally not found in state systems.

The maximum FECA benefit is based on 75% of the GS-15, Step 10 pay rate, without any locality adjustments whereas state maximums are generally based on state average wages or the worker's own pre-disability wage. For 2011, the annual salary at GS-15, Step 10, is $129,517, whereas the average federal salary for the executive branch in March 2011 was $74,915.[51] Thus, the maximum FECA benefit under the current system is higher than it would be if the FECA system based its maximum benefit level on average wages as is the case in the majority of the states.

The FECA basic benefit rate for total disability is two-thirds of the worker's pre-disability wage. Currently, 36 states and the District of Columbia have total disability benefit rates that are set at this level.[52] Benefits under the federal Longshore and Harbor Workers' Compensation Act are also set at two-thirds of the pre-disability wage. New Hampshire's benefit rate is 60% of the worker's pre-disability wage.

Currently, four states have total disability benefit rates that are based on pre-disability or average wages and that exceed the two-thirds standard. In New Jersey and Oklahoma, benefits are paid at 70% of the worker's wage at the time of injury whereas benefits in Texas are based on 75% of the worker's average wage. In Ohio, benefits are paid at 72% of the pre-disability wage for the first 12 weeks, then are reduced to the standard two-thirds rate.

Six states—Alaska, Connecticut, Iowa, Maine, Michigan, and Rhode Island—base benefits on net, rather than gross wages. It is generally not possible to compare these benefits to FECA benefits because of differences in tax rates that affect net income. Three states—Georgia, Pennsylvania, and Washington—have systems in which there is no direct comparison to the FECA total disability benefit rate.

Because of the augmented compensation provision of the FECA program, beneficiaries with dependents, including spouses, may receive total disability benefits at a rate of 75% of their pre-disability wages. No state pays augmented compensation for dependents, and the 75% benefit rate is higher than that paid by any comparable state workers' compensation system. Currently, more than 70% of FECA beneficiaries are receiving augmented compensation, and thus benefits at the rate of 75% of their pre-disability wages.[53]

One indication of the benefit generosity of the FECA program compared with state workers' compensation programs is the amount of disability benefits paid as a percentage of total program benefits. In 2009, disability benefits made up 49.1% of the total costs of benefits paid by state workers' compensation programs and 70.7% of total benefits paid by the FECA program.[54] Assuming that the types of injuries faced by federal employees and workers in the private and non-federal public sectors are not significantly different and that medical costs are also similar, this difference can be attributed to the generosity of FECA disability benefits, especially for higher-wage workers, compared with those offered by state workers' compensation systems.[55]

Legislative Activity

H.R. 2465 does not include provisions that would reduce the overall generosity of FECA benefits. Rather, H.R. 2465 would increase the continuation of pay period for federal employees serving in areas of armed conflict and increase funeral and disfigurement benefits. S. 1789 would eliminate augmented compensation except in certain cases of existing totally disabled beneficiaries, while increasing funeral and disfigurement benefits. The new U.S. Postal Service workers' compensation program that could be created under the provisions of H.R. 2309 would be prohibited from paying augmented compensation for dependents.

Program Administration

Insurance

The administration of state workers' compensation systems and the provision of insurance and benefits differs significantly from the FECA program. The FECA program does not involve any form of private insurance or private third-party administration of claims or benefits. Essentially, each federal entity acts like a self-insured employer with OWCP in the role of claims and benefit manager.

State workers' compensation benefits are generally provided by private insurance, state insurance funds, or through self insurance. All but four states—North Dakota, Ohio, Washington, and Wyoming—allow for private insurance. In Ohio and Washington, employers may either purchase insurance form the state fund or self-insure, whereas employers in North Dakota and Wyoming may not self-insure and must purchase coverage from the state fund. In 22 states, employers may purchase insurance from either a state fund or private carriers. All states except North Dakota and Wyoming allow self-insurance. Under the federal Longshore and Harbor Workers' Compensation Act, employers may purchase private insurance or self-insure.

Private insurance pays the majority of state workers' compensation benefits. In 2009, private insurers paid 55.6% of total state workers' compensation benefits whereas state funds paid 18.5% and self-insured firms paid 25.9%.[56] Thus, nearly three-quarters of all state workers' compensation benefits are paid through a system of third-party insurance rather than through the self-insurance model used by the FECA program.

Neither FECA reform legislation (H.R. 2465) nor postal reform legislation (S. 1789) would change the administration of FECA benefits or permit any type of private or third-party insurance. However, the postal reform legislation (H.R. 2309) would give broad discretion to the USPS to establish its own workers' compensation program, which could include private or third-party insurance.

Settlements

In 43 states and the District of Columbia, workers' compensation insurers or self-insured firms may enter into compromise and release settlements with claimants.[57] In these settlements, the insurer or firm agrees to pay the claimant lump-sum or periodic payment in exchange for being released from all future obligations under the claim. Compromise and release settlements are commonly used to avoid protracted disputes or litigation involving claims and are common in cases with potential for long-term payment of benefits. To accept a compromise and release settlement, the claimant generally must agree to forgo future benefits, which may be higher over his or her lifetime, in exchange for immediate payment. Insurers or firms must agree to forgo the possibility of lower future payments because of successfully controverting parts of a claim or the death, medical improvement, or return to work of the claimant, in exchange for clearing a claim off of their books with an immediate payment.

A 2010 study by the W.E. Upjohn Institute for Employment Research found that for 14 large states (California, Florida, Iowa, Illinois, Indiana, Louisiana, Massachusetts, Maryland, Michigan, North Carolina, Pennsylvania, Tennessee, Texas, and Wisconsin), for claims that originated between October 2003 and September 2004, and that had at least seven days of total lost work time, by March 2007, a median of 19% of these cases had been settled.[58]

Federal law does not provide for the settlement of FECA claims. Thus, the FECA program and FECA claimants are not able to take advantage of a tool used in approximately one-fifth of claims with the potential for long-term benefits, including the types of claims that are likely to result in beneficiaries receiving benefits well after retirement age.

Legislative Activity

The FECA reform legislation (H.R. 2465 and S. 1789) do not contain provisions that would permit the use of compromise and release settlements in the FECA program. Although the postal reform legislation (H.R. 2309) does not directly address the use of settlements, the broad authority given the USPS to create its own workers' compensation program could result in the use of settlements within that new program.

APPENDIX. FECA SCHEDULED BENEFITS

Table A-1. FECA Scheduled Benefits for Partial Disability Compensation

Loss of Use of Body System	Number of Weeks of Compensation
Scheduled benefits provided by statute [5 U.S.C. §8107(c)]	
Arm	312
Leg	288
Hand	244
Foot	205
Eye	106
Thumb	75
First finger	46
Great toe	38
Second finger	30

Loss of Use of Body System	Number of Weeks of Compensation
Third finger	25
Toe other than great toe	16
Fourth finger	15
Loss of hearing in one ear	52
Loss of hearing in both ears	200
Scheduled benefits provided by regulation [20 C.F.R. §10.404(a)]	
Breast	52
Kidney	156
Larynx	160
Lung	156
Penis	205
Testicle	52
Tongue	160
Ovary	52
Uterus or cervix	52
Vulva or vagina	52

Source: The Congressional Research Service.

Notes: Compensation is equal to two-thirds of the pre-disability wage of a single employee or 75% of the pre-disability wage of an employee with dependents for the number of weeks indicated.

End Notes

[1] Department of Labor, Office of Workers' Compensation Programs, *Annual Report to Congress: FY2009*, Washington, DC, April 27, 2011, p. 7.

[2] Ibid, p. 15.

[3] Act of May 4, 1882, ch. 117, 22 Stat. 55 (1882). In 1915 the United States Life Saving Service was merged with the Revenue Cutter Service to form the United States Coast Guard.

[4] Willis J. Nordlund, "The Federal Employees' Compensation Act," *Monthly Labor Review*, September 1991, p. 5 (Hereafter cited as Nordlund 1991.)

[5] U.S. Congress, House Committee on Education and Labor, Subcommittee on Safety and Compensation, *Amendments to Federal Employees' Compensation Act*, hearings on H.R. 1196 and other bills to amend the Federal Employees'Compensation Act, 86th Cong., 2nd sess., February 10, 23, 24 and March 8, 23, 24, 1960 (Washington: GPO, 1960), p. 124.

[6] Coverage for occupational illnesses was added to the FECA program in 1924 by P.L. 68-195.

[7] U.S. Congress, House Committee on the Judiciary, *Compensation of Government Employees Suffering Injuries While on Duty*, report to accompany H.R. 15316, 64th Cong., 2nd sess., May 11, 1916, H. Rept. 64-678 (Washington: GPO, 1916), p. 7.

[8] Ibid., p. 9.

[9] Ibid., p. 8.

[10] U.S. Congress, Senate Committee on the Judiciary, *Accident Compensation to Government Employees*, hearing on S. 2846, 64th Cong., 1st sess., February 26, 1916 (Washington: GPO, 1916), p. 27.

[11] Ibid.

[12] U.S. Congress, House Committee on Education and Labor, *Amendments to Federal Employees' Compensation Act*, report to accompany H.R. 3141, 81st Cong., 1st sess., June 6, 1949, H. Rept. 81-729 (Washington: GPO, 1949), p. 23, hereafter cited as H.Rept. 81-729; and U.S. Congress, Senate Labor and Public Welfare, *Amendments to Federal Employees' Compensation Act*, report to accompany H.R. 3141, 81st Cong., 1st sess., August 4, 1949, S.Rept. 81-836 (Washington: GPO, 1949), p. 29, hereafter cited as S.Rept. 81-836.

[13] Nordlund 1991, p. 10.

[14] The Longshore and Harbor Workers' Compensation Act Program was created in 1927. For additional information on the Longshore and Harbor Workers' Compensation Act, see CRS Report R41506, *The Longshore and Harbor Workers' Compensation Act (LHWCA): Overview of Workers' Compensation for Certain Private-Sector Maritime Workers*, by Scott Szymendera.

[15] H.Rept. 81-279, p. 11; and S.Rept. 81-836, p. 20.

[16] U.S. Congress, House Committee on Education and Labor, Special Subcommittee, *Federal Employees' Compensation Act Amendments of 1949*, hearing on H.R. 3191 and companion bills, 81st Cong., 1st sess., April 11-13 and May 2, 1949.

[17] Ibid.

[18] H.Rept. 81-279, p. 16; and S.Rept. 81-836, p. 24.

[19] For additional information on the Federal Tort Claims Act, see CRS Report 95-717, *Federal Tort Claims Act (FTCA)*, by Vivian S. Chu.

[20] H.Rept. 81-279, p. 14; and S.Rept. 81-836, p. 23.

[21] U.S. Congress, House Committee on Education and Labor, *Federal Employees' Compensation Act Amendments of1960*, report to accompany H.R. 12383, 86th Cong., 2nd sess., June 2, 1960, H.Rept. 86-1743 (Washington: GPO, 1960), p. 3; and U.S. Congress, Senate Committee on Labor and Public Welfare, *Federal Employees' Compensation Act Amendments of 1960*, report to accompany H.R. 12383, 86th Cong., 2nd sess., August 27, 1960, S.Rept. 86-1924 (Washington: GPO, 1960), p. 3.

[22] U.S. Congress, Senate Committee on Labor and Public Welfare, *Federal Employees' Compensation Act Amendments of 1966*, report to accompany H.R. 10721, 89th Cong., 2nd sess., June 16, 1966, S.Rept. 89-1285, p. 3.

[23] The current cost-of-living adjustment is made each year on March 1 and is based on changes in the Consumer Price Index for Urban Wage Earners and Clerical Workers (CPI-W; all items-United States city average) as measured in December of each year.

[24] U.S. Congress, Senate Committee on Labor and Public Welfare, *Federal Employees' Compensation Act of 1970*, report to accompany H.R. 13871, 93rd Cong., 2nd sess., August 8, 1974, S.Rept. 93-1081 (Washington: GPO, 1974), pp. 3-4, hereafter cited as S.Rept. 93-1081; and U.S. General Accounting Office, *Need for a Faster Way to Pay Compensation Claims to Disabled Federal Employees*, B-157593, November 21, 1973, p. 1.

[25] S.Rept. 93-1081, p. 7.

[26] President's Commission on the United States Postal Service, *Embracing the Future: Making the Tough Choices to Preserve Universal Mail Service*, Report of the President's Commission on the United States Postal Service, July 31, 2003, p. 134.

[27] See, for example, U.S. Congress, House Committee on Oversight and Government Reform, Subcommittee on Federal Workforce, Post Office, and the District of Columbia, *A Call to Arms: A Review of Benefits for Deployed Federal Employees*, hearing, 111th Cong., 1st sess., September 16, 2009; and U.S. Congress, Senate Committee on Homeland Security and Governmental Affairs, Subcommittee on Oversight of Government Management, the Federal Workforce, and the District of Columbia, *Deployed Federal Civilians: Advancing Security and Opportunity in Afghanistan*, hearing, 111th Cong., 2nd sess., April 14, 2010.

[28] United States Postal Service, Office of Inspector General, *Postal Service Workers' Compensation Program Audit Report*, Report Number HR-AR-11-007, Washington, DC, September 30, 2011, p. 8.

[29] Ishita Sengupta, Virginia Reno, and John F. Burton, Jr., *Workers' Compensation: Benefits, Coverage, and Costs, 2009*, National Academy of Social Insurance, Washington, DC, August 2011, p. 7.,(Hereafter cited as Sengupta et al., 2011.) Direct administrative costs are OWCP's costs of administering the FECA program. Indirect administrative costs are for activities, such as investigations or legal support, outside of OWCP.

[30] Certain groups, including federal jurors, Peace Corps volunteers, and Civil Air Patrol members, are not eligible for continuation of pay.

[31] The list of FECA scheduled benefits are provided in statute at 5 U.S.C. Section 8107(c) and in regulation at 20 C.F.R. Section 10.404(a).

[32] A copy of the current OWCP medical fee schedule can be found on the Department of Labor website at http://www.dol.gov/owcp/regs/feeschedule/fee.htm.

[33] Some federal employees, such as Foreign Service Officers or employees of non-appropriated fund instrumentalities, are covered by federal retirement systems other than CSRS or FERS. For additional information on the more than 30 types of federal retirement systems, see U.S. General Accounting Office, *Public Pensions: Summary of Federal Pension Plan Data*, GAO/AIMD-96-6, February 1996. For additional information on the FERS and CSRS, see CRS Report 98-810, *Federal Employees' Retirement System: Benefits and Financing*, by Katelin P. Isaacs.

[34] For additional information on the TSP, see CRS Report RL30387, *Federal Employees' Retirement System: The Role of the Thrift Savings Plan*, by Katelin P. Isaacs.

[35] The only payroll deductions taken from FECA benefits are for Federal Employee Health Benefits (FEHB) and basic, optional, and post-retirement basic life insurance if the employee is enrolled in these programs.

[36] P.L. 108-92.

[37] For additional information on disability retirement under CSRS and FERS, see CRS Report RS22838, *Disability Retirement for Federal Employees*, by Katelin P. Isaacs.

[38] 42 U.S.C. §424a.

[39] For additional information on the SSDI program, see CRS Report RL32279, *Primer on Disability Benefits: Social Security Disability Insurance (SSDI) and Supplemental Security Income (SSI)*, by Umar Moulta-Ali.

[40] U.S. Congress, House Committee on Oversight and Government Reform, Subcommittee on Federal Workforce, U.S. Postal Service, and Labor Policy, *FECA: A Fair Approach*, 112th Cong., 1st sess., April 13, 2011; U.S. Congress, House Committee on Education and the Workforce, Subcommittee on Workforce Protections, *Reviewing Workers' Compensation for Federal Employees*, 112th Cong., 1st sess., May 12, 2011; and U.S. Congress, Senate Committee on Homeland Security and Governmental Affairs, Subcommittee on Oversight of Government Management, the Federal Workforce, and the District of Columbia, *Examining the Federal Workers' Compensation Program for Injured Employees*, 112th Cong., 1st sess., July 26, 2011.

[41] Department of Labor, Occupational Safety and Health Administration, *Federal Injury and Illness Statistics for Fiscal Year 2010*, http://www.osha.gov/dep/fap/statistics/fedprgms_stats10_final.html#footnote4a.

[42] Department of Labor, Office of Workers' Compensation Programs, *FY2010 End of Year LPD Report for All Government*, http://www.dol.gov/owcp/dfec/share/lpd/FY20104thQtr/All Government.htm.

[43] The total number of lost production days is calculated based on June 2010 employment data compiled by the Occupational Safety and Health Administration (OSHA) from various sources and posted on its website at http://www.osha.gov/dep/fap/statistics/fedprgms_stats10_final.html#footnote1 and on end-of-fiscal year injury data reported by the Department of Labor on its website at http://www.dol.gov/owcp/dfec/share/lpd/FY2010

4thQtr/AllGovernment.htm. Because the number of federal employees fluctuates throughout the year, and because no one agency of the federal government collects data on employment in the executive, legislative, and judicial branches of the government, the calculated number of total lost production days must be treated as an estimate. The estimated number of lost work years is calculated based on 260 work days in a work year.

[44] Department of Labor, Office of Workers' Compensation Programs, *Annual Report to Congress: FY2009*, Washington, DC, April 27, 2011, p. 11. A chargeback year runs from July 1 to June 30.

[45] U.S. Congress, Senate Committee on Homeland Security and Governmental Affairs, Subcommittee on Oversight of Government Management, the Federal Workforce, and the District of Columbia, *Examining the Federal Workers' Compensation Program for Injured Employees*, 112th Cong., 1st sess., July 26, 2011, (statement of Gary Steinberg, Acting Director, Office of Workers' Compensation Programs).

[46] U.S. Postal Service Office of Inspector General, *Postal Service Workers' Compensation Program: Audit Report*, Report Number HR-AR-11-007, September 30, 2011, p. 1.

[47] S. Rept. 93-1081, p. 7.

[48] Sengupta, et al., 2011, pp. 86-95.

[49] For additional information on the Social Security retirement age, see CRS Report R41962, *Fact Sheet: The Social Security Retirement Age*, by Alison M. Shelton.

[50] This letter is available on the website of the House Committee on Education and the Workforce at http://edworkforce.house.gov/UploadedFiles/GAO_FECA_July_2011.pdf.

[51] Information on the GS-15 salary rate taken from the website of the Office of Personnel Management (OPM) at http://www.opm.gov/oca/11tables/html/gs.asp. Information on average federal salary taken form the OPM FedScope system online at http://www.fedscope.opm.gov/.

[52] Sengupta et al., 2011, pp. 86-95.

[53] U.S. Congress, Senate Committee on Homeland Security and Governmental Affairs, Subcommittee on Oversight of Government Management, the Federal Workforce, and the District of Columbia, *Examining the Federal Workers' Compensation Program for Injured Employees*, 112th Cong., 1st sess., July 26, 2011 (statement of Gary Steinberg,Acting Director, Office of Workers' Compensation Programs).

[54] Sengupta et al., 2011, pp. 24-25.

[55] This conclusion is supported by Sengupta et al. who state "The share of benefits for medical care is lower than in most state programs because federal cash benefits, particularly for higher-wage workers, replace a larger share of pre-injury wages than is the case in most state programs" (Sengupta et al., 2011, p. 78).

[56] Sengupta et al., 2011, pp. 24-25.

[57] Peter S. Barth, *Compromise and Release Settlements in Workers' Compensation: Final Report*, W.E. Upjohn Institute for Employment Research, report prepared for the State of Washington, Department of Labor and Industries, December 21, 2010, pp. 44-45, http://research.upjohn.org/reports/178/.

[58] Ibid., p. 43.

In: The Federal Employees' Compensation Act ISBN: 978-1-62081-729-2
Editors: A. K. James and F. E. Davis

Chapter 2

FEDERAL EMPLOYEES' COMPENSATION ACT: BENEFITS FOR RETIREMENT-AGE BENEFICIARIES *

United States Government Accountability Office

In 2010, the Federal Employees' Compensation Act (FECA)[1] program paid approximately $2.8 billion in total cash and medical benefits to federal employees who sustained injuries or illnesses while performing federal duties; about $1.9 billion of that was for cash benefits.[2] U.S. Postal Service (USPS) has the largest number of FECA beneficiaries. The Department of Labor (Labor), which oversees the program, categorizes FECA beneficiaries into groups based on their ability to work, length of time receiving benefits, and type of injury. There are some beneficiaries who have been receiving benefits for longer than 90 days, and are completely unable to work. We refer to this group as long-term, full-time beneficiaries. Because there are no time or age limits for receiving FECA benefits, long-term, full-time beneficiaries include people at or older than retirement age.

We examined (1) the characteristics and associated compensation costs of long-term, full-time FECA beneficiaries, for USPS and non-USPS employees; (2) how wage compensation benefits for retirement-age, long-term, full-time FECA beneficiaries compare with federal retirees' annuities (not including

---

* This is an edited, reformatted and augmented version of the GAO-12-309R Congressional Committees, dated February 6, 2012.

USPS employees); and (3) the experiences of states that limit state workers' compensation benefits for workers at retirement age. For the first question, we could include USPS employees because Labor provided us with data on FECA beneficiaries for all federal agencies, including USPS. However, we could not include USPS employees in answering the second question. Our analysis required determining the work histories for FECA beneficiaries and retired annuitants, using an Office of Personnel Management (OPM) database to obtain these work histories. USPS employees are not included in the OPM database.[3] We subsequently obtained data from USPS; however, the data were missing a significant amount of information necessary to determine the work histories of USPS employees for the years covered by our analysis.[4] According to USPS officials, they changed data systems in 1995 and some key data were not available.

To determine characteristics and compensation costs of long-term, full-time FECA beneficiaries, we analyzed data from the Department of Labor's FECA claimant database for chargeback year 2010.[5] (References to FECA data in 2010 from this point forward refer to the chargeback year.) We conducted this analysis for these FECA beneficiaries, using their full retirement age as set forth in the Social Security Act.[6] To compare FECA benefit levels with federal retirees' annuities, we conducted an analysis of retirees who were at least 55 years old and long-term, full-time FECA beneficiaries of the same age who did not work for the USPS who were covered by the Civil Service Retirement System (CSRS) in 2010.[7] We focused on this age group of FECA beneficiaries because the minimum age of retirement eligibility under CSRS is 55 years old and using the lower age increased the number of individuals we could include in our analysis. We compared the FECA benefits to the annuities of federal retirees who were similar in terms of demographics, agencies they worked for, occupations, retirement plans, incomes prior to injury or retirement, and years of federal service at the point of the FECA beneficiaries' date of injury. The analysis did not distinguish between FECA beneficiaries who have no dependents, and received 66-2/3 percent of their preinjury salaries and those beneficiaries with dependents who received 75 percent of their preinjury salaries. Because FECA benefits are not taxed, and in order to make those benefits comparable to annuities that are taxed, our analysis accounted for the effects of federal and state income taxes on retirees' annuities.[8] Our comparison did not include individuals receiving part-time Loss of Wage Earning Capacity (LWEC) benefits. These individuals do not receive full disability benefits from FECA, because it has been determined that they are capable of working part-time or with restrictions.[9] For our review of the state workers' compensation programs, we conducted case studies in four states that limit these benefits by retirement age—Kentucky, Minnesota, Montana, and Tennessee—out of a total of eight states that have age-based workers' compensation limits, as identified by the Workers' Compensation Research Institute. We interviewed workers' compensation board officials and private sector attorneys who specialize in workers' compensation about their experiences in managing these programs, specifically relating to retirement-age limitations.

Enclosures I and II contain a detailed description of our scope and methodology.

We requested comments on a draft of this report from Labor, OPM, and USPS. The agencies' comments are discussed at the end of this report.

We conducted this performance audit from February 2011 through February 2012 in accordance with generally accepted government auditing standards. Those standards require that we plan and perform the audit to obtain sufficient, appropriate evidence to provide a reasonable basis for our findings and conclusions based on our audit objectives. We believe that the evidence obtained provides a reasonable basis for our findings and conclusions based on our audit objectives.

BACKGROUND

Labor's Division of Federal Employees' Compensation in the Office of Workers' Compensation Programs (OWCP) administers the FECA program. This program provides cash benefits and medical benefits to federal employees who suffer temporary or permanent disabilities resulting from work-related injuries or diseases. FECA cash benefits include payments for wages lost when employees cannot work because of work-related disabilities due to traumatic injuries or occupational diseases; schedule awards for loss of, or loss of use of, a body part or function; death benefits for survivors; and burial allowances. Medical benefits include vocational rehabilitation and medical care for injured workers. FECA cash benefits are not taxed.

OWCP charges agencies for whom injured employees worked for benefits provided. These agencies subsequently reimburse Labor's Employees' Compensation Fund from their next annual appropriation. USPS and the Department of Veterans Affairs have the largest number of FECA beneficiaries, as shown in table 1.[10]

Table 1. Number of FECA Beneficiaries per Agency in 2010

Agency	All FECA beneficiaries	
	Number	Percentage
USPS	130,483	43
Department of Veterans Affairs	26,157	9
Department of Homeland Security	25,408	8
Navy	19,919	6
Army	19,852	6
Air Force	12,728	4
Department of Justice	11,001	4
Department of Agriculture	10,691	3
Department of the Interior	9,205	3
Defense agencies[a]	6,101	2
Other agencies[b]	35,360	12
Total	**306,905**	**100**

Source: GAO analysis of Labor data.

[a] Defense Agencies covered include the Defense Contract Audit Agency, Defense Logistics Agency, and the Defense Contract Management Agency, among others.

[b] The remaining agencies listed each have less than 2 percent of the total number of beneficiaries receiving workers' compensation benefits, and fewer than 5,275 beneficiaries each.

Eligible workers with temporary or permanent total disabilities who have no spouse or dependent generally receive wage-loss compensation equal to 66-2/3 percent of their salary at injury. Those with a spouse or dependent receive 75 percent. OWCP can reduce wage-loss compensation based on employees' wage-earning capacities when Labor determines they are capable of working again. OWCP provides wage-loss compensation until claimants can return to work in either their original positions or other suitable positions that meet medical work restrictions.

Claimants are not allowed to receive FECA benefits at the same time they receive certain other federal disability or retirement benefits.[11] For example, claimants are not allowed to receive both FECA wage-loss-compensation payments and disability payments from the Department of Veterans Affairs for the same injury. Further, claimants cannot receive federal retirement benefits, such as CSRS or Federal Employees' Retirement System (FERS) benefits, paid through OPM concurrently with FECA wage-loss benefits; they must elect to receive one or the other. However, the law authorizing FECA does not require beneficiaries to "retire" at a certain age by, for example, transitioning to a federal pension program like CSRS. They can continue receiving FECA wage-loss compensation payments for as long as they remain unable to work due to a workplace injury.

Typically, federal workers participate in one of two retirement systems, which are administered by OPM: CSRS or FERS.[12] CSRS covers most civilian federal employees who were hired before 1984. Under CSRS, employees generally do not pay Social Security taxes or earn Social Security benefits. Federal employees first hired in 1984 or later are covered by FERS.[13]

Concerns that beneficiaries remain in the FECA program past traditional retirement age have led to two types of proposals to change the program. As we have discussed in previous work, one type of proposal would convert FECA benefits to regular federal employee retirement benefits at retirement age. A second type of proposal would convert FECA benefits to a retirement-age FECA benefit.[14]

States also administer individual state workers' compensation programs for injured workers, but FECA and the state programs differ in important ways. For example, the FECA program provides coverage for injured workers from one fund, administered by Labor. In contrast, in states, multiple private insurers generally pay most claims, and state programs typically provide coverage for both private and public sector workers. In addition, state compensation awards may often be appealed to state courts. In contrast, FECA is intended to be nonadversarial and remedial in nature.[15]

SUMMARY

In 2010, 31,880—or 10 percent—of all FECA beneficiaries were long-term, full-time beneficiaries and 10,873 of those—or 34 percent—were at full retirement age, as defined under the Social Security Act. Of the $1.9 billion total in cash benefits paid to FECA beneficiaries, over half (58 percent) went to long-term, full-time beneficiaries. Of that half, long-term, full-time beneficiaries at or above full Social Security retirement age received 21 percent. This analysis covered all FECA beneficiaries, including USPS and non-USPS employees.

Compared to their federal CSRS retired counterparts, non-USPS long-term, full-time FECA beneficiaries typically received higher benefits in 2010. The median annual FECA benefit of $35,614 was about 26 percent higher than the median annual annuity received by retirees, which was $28,289, after adjusting for the effects of taxes. The difference between FECA benefits and CSRS annuities is typically larger when the FECA beneficiary was injured after fewer years of service. The differences between annual FECA and CSRS benefits in our comparison are largely explained by the benefit calculation formulas used for each set of benefits. The CSRS formula generally awards a smaller percentage of salary than the FECA formula for most workers, except those with long tenure. It is important to note that our finding regarding the difference in benefits levels does not allow us to conclude whether such a difference exists for USPS employees or for current or future annuitants under FERS, a population that is increasing given that FERS covers federal employees first hired in 1984 or later. USPS employees were not included in this analysis because USPS could not provide sufficient data to reliably determine its employees' work histories for the years covered by our analysis.

We examined the experiences of four states that limit state workers' compensation benefits based on retirement age: Kentucky, Minnesota, Montana, and Tennessee. State officials and attorneys in those states highlighted several aspects of their experiences with these provisions, including cost savings, legal challenges, and financial hardships for some beneficiaries. For example, a workers' compensation board official from Kentucky stated there has been a decrease in workers' compensation costs since the retirement-age limitation went into effect; however, their office could not attribute the savings to this provision because they lack statistical data since private insurance carriers pay the benefits rather than the state.

In 2010, Long-Term, Full-Time FECA Beneficiaries, Many at Retirement Age, Received More Than Half of All FECA Cash Benefits

A sizable portion of FECA beneficiaries who received cash benefits16 are long-term, full-time beneficiaries.[17] Many of these were at or above full Social Security retirement age. Of the 306,905 individuals who received FECA benefits in 2010, about 79,261 received cash benefits (see figure 1).[18] Somewhat less than half (31,880) of these recipients were classified as long-term, full-time beneficiaries.· Among long-term, full-time beneficiaries, about 34 percent (10,873) were at retirement age and most were injured more than 20 years ago.[19] This analysis covered all FECA beneficiaries, including USPS and non-USPS employees.

Long-term, full-time beneficiaries received 58 percent of total cash benefits in 2010. In addition, 21 percent of all cash benefits was paid to long-term, full-time, retirement-age beneficiaries, who were 3 percent of all FECA beneficiaries, as shown in figure 2.

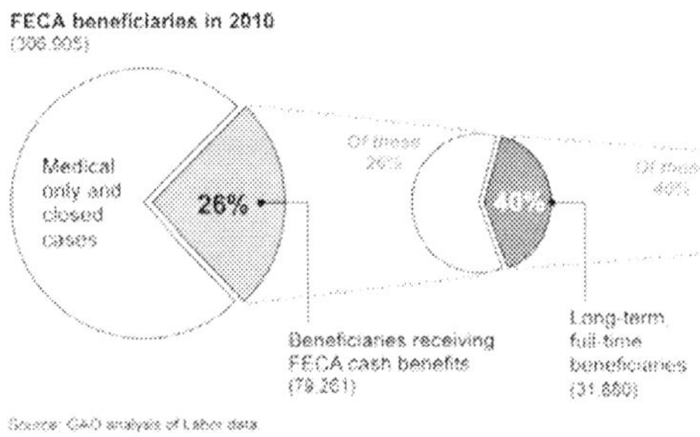

Note: Because of the way Labor maintains its data, it is not possible to know whether an individual whose case closed in 2010 did or did not receive cash benefits. For additional information on FECA case status and compensation, see enclosure IV.

Figure 1. Number of FECA Beneficiaries Receiving FECA Cash Benefits in 2010.

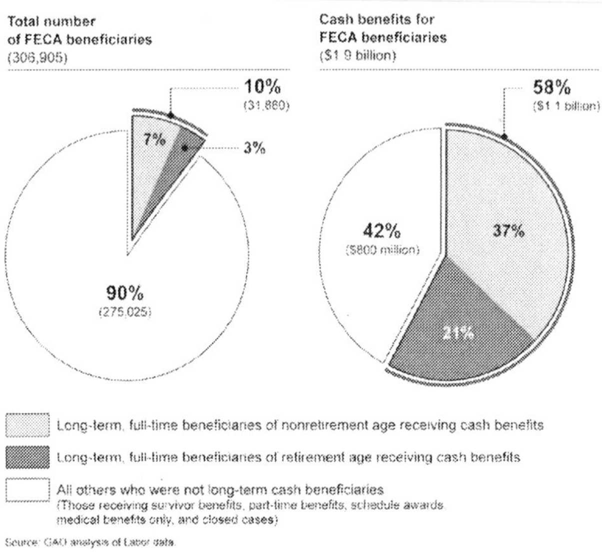

Note: Because of the way Labor maintains its data, it is not possible to know whether a case closed in 2010 did or did not receive cash benefits. For additional information on FECA case status and compensation, see enclosure IV.

Figure 2. FECA Beneficiaries and Cash Benefits Received in 2010.

Although long-term, full-time beneficiaries received over half of all cash benefits paid in 2010, most of these individuals (89 percent) received less than $50,000 per year in cash benefits (see enc. IV, table 18). The median annual cash benefit was about $34,000 per year. A small number of FECA beneficiaries received more than $100,000 in benefits in 2010. That year, 116 individuals (or less than 1 percent of long-term, full-time beneficiaries) received more than $100,000.[20] USPS employees made up about one-third of these individuals receiving over $100,000. While our analysis shows that about one-third of long-term, full-time beneficiaries were retirement age, a number of beneficiaries were between the ages of 50 and 59 and approaching retirement age (see enc. IV, table 15).

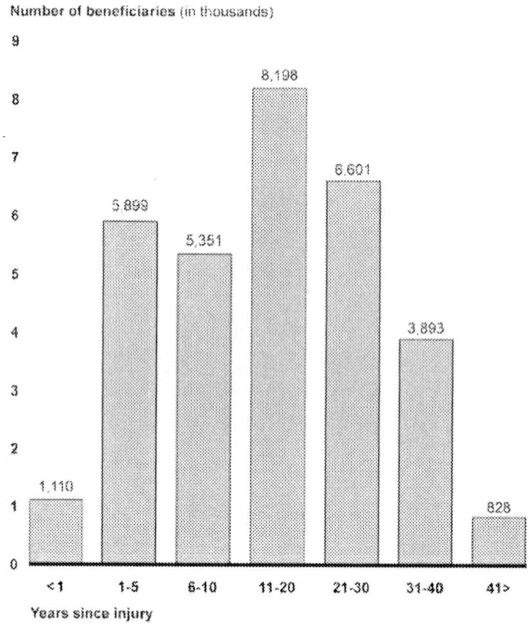

Note: Labor does not maintain this data in a way that would allow us to determine the cumulative total amount of time a FECA beneficiary has received benefits since the date of injury.

Figure 3. Years from the Date of Injury for Long-Term, Full-Time Beneficiaries in 2010.

We calculated that one-third of long-term, full-time beneficiaries were injured more than 20 years ago, as shown in figure 3. Labor's data system is not designed in a way that would allow us to determine the cumulative total amount of time a person has been receiving FECA benefits. Given these constraints, we calculated how long long-term, full-time beneficiaries had been receiving benefits from their date of injury. This calculation does not account for any possible breaks in benefits during that time—e.g., if an employee returned to work. As a result, this proxy probably overestimates the time they have been receiving FECA benefits of any kind.Enclosure IV provides detailed information on the characteristics of three groups: (1) all FECA beneficiaries, (2) long-term, full-time FECA beneficiaries, and (3) long-term, full-time retirement-age FECA beneficiaries.

In 2010, Long-Term, Full-Time, Non-USPS, FECA Beneficiaries Typically Received Cash Benefits That Were Higher Than CSRS Annuities

In this analysis, we compared non-USPS long-term, full-time FECA beneficiaries who were covered by CSRS and at least 55 years old to an equivalent group of actual CSRS recipients of the same age.[21] Enclosure II provides more detailed information on our comparison of the benefits and annuities for the non-USPS FECA beneficiaries and CSRS retirees.

Annual Non-USPS FECA Cash Benefits Were Typically Higher than Federal CSRS Annuities

In 2010, the FECA benefits of long-term, full-time beneficiaries we analyzed were typically higher than the retirement annuities of CSRS retirees (see table 2).[22] These FECA beneficiaries received a median annual benefit of $35,614, while the comparison group of CSRS retirees received a median annual annuity of $29,196, before adjusting for taxes. The median FECA benefit was $7,325 higher than the median annual annuity received by retirees, which was $28,289, after adjusting for taxes.[23]

Table 2. Comparison of Median Non-USPS Annual FECA Cash Benefits and CSRS Annuities

	Median annual FECA benefit	Median annual CSRS annuity before taxes	Median annual CSRS annuity after taxes	Difference between median annual FECA benefit and CSRS annuity after taxes
All long-term, full-time FECA beneficiaries	$35,614[a]	$29,196	$28,289	$7,324
Years of service [b]				
Less than 10	$29,256	$16,806	$16,806[c]	$12,450
10 to 19	$32,911	$23,226	$22,956	$9,956
20 to 29	$38,303	$32,244	$31,007	$7,296
30 or more	$43,932	$43,020	$40,240	$3,692

Source: GAO analysis of Labor and OPM data.

Notes: Statistics on FECA benefits apply to cash benefits received by beneficiaries who were at least 55 years old and covered by CSRS. Statistics on annuities apply to CSRS retirees who were at least 55 years old. Due to the limited historical data available on federal employees, both groups include only employees who had electronic records between 1988 and 2010 and were not USPS employees.

[a] This analysis included only wage-loss replacement payments for long-term, full-time beneficiaries. Schedule awards and survivor benefits are not included.

[b] We matched the FECA beneficiary and the annuitant on equivalent years of service at the point of the FECA beneficiary's date of injury.

[c] At this income level, many of the recipients had no tax liability.

The difference between FECA benefits and CSRS annuities is typically larger when the FECA beneficiary was injured after fewer years of service. The median annual FECA benefit for beneficiaries with 10 or fewer years of service when injured was $12,450 more than the median CSRS annuity. In contrast, the median annual FECA benefit for beneficiaries with 30 or more years of service when injured—and thus closer to retirement—was $3,692 more than the median CSRS annuity.[24]

The differences between annual FECA and CSRS benefits in our comparison are largely explained by the benefit calculation formulas used for each set of benefits. The FECA formula awards 66 2/3 percent (for individuals) or 75 percent (for those with dependents) of the salary at time of injury. The benefit also increases over time by the FECA cost of living adjustment (COLA).[25] The CSRS formula generally awards a smaller percentage of salary than the FECA formula for most workers, except those with long tenure. Also, FECA beneficiaries with a dependent have higher benefits, while the provision of a joint and survivor annuity under CSRS generally provides a survivor benefit that lowers the amount received by the beneficiary (thus increasing the differences between FECA benefits and retirement annuities). Other factors may affect such comparisons, as well. By contrast, as seen in table 2, differences due to taxes are relatively small.

See enclosure III for detailed information on the differences in FECA and retirement benefits and annuities for non-USPS long-term, full-time beneficiaries and non-USPS retirees, with respect to differences in each of the following factors: years of service at the time of injury, years since exit from federal service, maximum prior income, and age in 2010.

SELECTED STATES THAT SET AGE LIMITS FOR WORKERS' COMPENSATION PROGRAMS REPORTED SAVINGS, LEGAL CHALLENGES, AND FINANCIAL HARDSHIPS FOR SOME BENEFICIARIES

We examined experiences in four states—Kentucky, Minnesota, Montana, and Tennessee—that limit workers' compensation benefits for wage-loss compensation based on retirement age.[26] These states generally restrict wage-loss benefits for workers who reach retirement age if they have an injury rated as a "permanent total disability"—i.e., a condition that prevents a return to work.[27] Kentucky, Montana, and Tennessee consider workers "retired"[28] when they are eligible for full retirement benefits under the Social Security Act.[29] The remaining state—Minnesota—presumes people are "retired from the labor market" upon reaching 67 years of age. However, that person may present evidence to challenge this presumption, such as proof that they were already working past age 67 when injured, according to a state official. (See table 3.)

Stakeholders we interviewed from the four states highlighted several aspects of their experiences regarding retirement-age limitations on workers' compensation benefits, including cost savings, legal challenges, and financial challenges for beneficiaries. Stakeholders included state workers' compensation board officials and private attorneys who specialize in workers' compensation cases.

Table 3. Retirement-Age Limits of Wage-loss Benefits for Permanent Total Disability in Selected State Workers' Compensation Programs

State	Retirement-age Limitations	Year enacted
Kentucky	Wage-loss benefits end when claimant qualifies for full retirement benefits under the Social Security Act or 2 years after the claimant's last injury, whichever is later.	1996
Minnesota	Wage-loss benefits end when claimant reaches age 67.	1996
Montana	Wage-loss benefits end when claimant receives or is eligible to receive full retirement benefits under the Social Security Act or alternative retirement system.	1981
Tennessee	• Wage-loss benefits end when claimant is, by age, eligible for full retirement benefits under the Social Security Act. • If a person is injured after age 60, wage-loss benefits continue for a maximum of 260 weeks (5 years), with the compensation rate reduced by half of the amount of any Social Security benefits received during the period of the award.[a]	1994

Source: State workers' compensation officials.

[a] A person after age 60 may receive a maximum of 260 weeks for any work injury, whether it is permanent total or permanent partial disability. Since permanent total disability benefits end with full retirement eligibility, many persons older than 60 elect permanent partial disability even if they are unable to return to work with the preinjury employer, according to a state workers' compensation official.

Cost Savings

Workers' compensation board officials from three of the states said that adding the retirement-age limitation lowered costs, but officials from two states could not quantify the savings. For example, a Minnesota workers' compensation official said the state made many other changes simultaneously to its workers' compensation program, such as setting a new type of maximum weekly rate for all wage-loss benefits and a new minimum weekly benefit rate for permanent total disability benefits; consequently, the workers' compensation office was unable to attribute savings to a single provision. A workers' compensation board official from Kentucky stated there has been a decrease in workers' compensation costs since the retirement-age limitation went into effect; however, the official's office could not attribute the savings to this provision because it lacked statistical data since private insurance carriers pay the benefits rather than the state. A workers' compensation official from Montana told us that the official's office did not calculate the cost impact of the retirement-age limitation; however, the official referred us to a 2005 report by the state's audit organization that estimated that repealing the retirement-age limitation would cost the Montana workers' compensation fund $228 million to $302 million for nonsettled permanent total disability claims that arose between 1981 and 2004.[30]

Legal Challenges

Private attorneys from three of the states said that legal challenges to the retirement-age limitation have been raised in their states, but the courts have generally upheld the retirement-age limitation. For example, according to attorneys in Montana, in one case the state's supreme court did not find a rational basis to overturn the retirement-age limitation for workers receiving permanent total disability benefits. In another case, however, the court established that workers receiving permanent partial disability benefits can continue to receive them past retirement age. The state courts in Kentucky and Tennessee have upheld the constitutionality of the retirement-age limitation of workers' compensation benefits, according to private attorneys from those states.

Financial Hardships for Some Beneficiaries

Private attorneys from all four states told us that individuals whose benefits end when they reach retirement age can face financial challenges. For example, attorneys in Kentucky said some people work into their 80s because they need the income and cannot afford to retire. These attorneys said that if such workers suffer a work-related injury at age 67, they potentially lose 15 to 20 years of earnings, even though their wage-loss benefits would cover only 2 years. In addition, the Kentucky attorneys noted that while wage-loss benefits continue for older beneficiaries who are ineligible for full retirement Social Security benefits, wage-loss benefits cease for a claimant who qualifies for even a small amount of Social Security retirement benefits.

Agency Comments

We provided a draft of this report to Labor, OPM, and USPS for review and comment. In its comments, USPS said that under current statute, FECA provides benefits greater than those provided under the traditional federal retirement systems for injured workers who are retirement age. USPS added that it has become imperative that this matter be addressed through legislative change. Labor provided technical comments, which we incorporated in the report as appropriate. OPM indicated that it did not have any comments.

Andrew Sherrill
Director, Education, Workforce and Income Security Issues

Phillip Herr
Managing Director, Physical Infrastructure Issues
Enclosures

List of Congressional Committees

The Honorable Susan M. Collins
Ranking Member
Committee on Homeland Security and Government Affairs
United States Senate

The Honorable Thomas R. Carper
Chairman
Subcommittee on Federal Financial Management,
Government Information, Federal Services, and International Security
Committee on Homeland Security and Governmental Affairs
United States Senate

The Honorable Claire McCaskill
Chair
Ad Hoc Subcommittee on Contracting Oversight
Committee on Homeland Security and Government Affairs
United States Senate

The Honorable Tom Coburn
Ranking Member

Permanent Subcommittee on Investigations
Committee on Homeland Security and Government Affairs
United States Senate

The Honorable Darrell Issa
Chairman
Committee on Oversight and Government Reform
House of Representatives

ENCLOSURE I. DETAILS ON AUDIT SCOPE AND METHODOLOGY

To determine the characteristics and benefits for Federal Employees' Compensation Act (FECA) beneficiaries, we collected data from Department of Labor's (Labor) Integrated Federal Employees' Compensation System (iFECS), FECA's claimant database for chargeback year 201031 to calculate the number of beneficiaries by age and length of time receiving benefits from their injury date, including those in the program past Social Security full retirement age. Because Labor's iFECS system does not track the length of time each beneficiary was receiving benefits, we used injury date as a proxy. We also calculated and reported FECA benefits based on various recipient characteristics, such as agency, benefit type, as well as total costs associated with cash benefits for FECA beneficiaries who are past Social Security full retirement age. We assessed the reliability of the data by (1) electronically testing required data elements, (2) reviewing existing information about the data and the system that produced them, and (3) interviewing agency officials knowledgeable about the data. We determined that the data we reviewed were reliable for the purposes of this report.

To determine if FECA beneficiaries' benefits were higher or lower than federal retirees' annuities, we assembled data from Labor's iFECS and the Office of Personnel Management's (OPM) annuitant database and Central Personnel Data File (CPDF), a central personnel database that has reliable longitudinal data starting in fiscal year 1988. Our analysis focused on long-term, full-time FECA beneficiaries who were covered by Civil Service Retirement System (CSRS). We excluded FECA recipients who were part of the FERS retirement system, because there are more CSRS employee annuitants currently receiving annuities. We excluded those FECA beneficiaries and retirees from our analysis who were not working after 1988.

We excluded U.S. Postal Service (USPS) FECA beneficiaries from our analysis because USPS could not provide reliable, comparable data on its employees. For example, we needed a service computation date to determine the length of service for annuitants.[32] However, the service computation data we received from USPS for the period 1988 to 2010 were missing these data for 16 percent to 90 percent of employees, depending on the year. Furthermore, data in 1988 and 1989 were missing a significant amount of information we needed.

Exclusion of USPS employees and our selection criteria left us with approximately 4,000 non-USPS FECA beneficiaries and approximately 301,000 CSRS annuitants. We accounted for federal and state taxes on retirees' annuities using the NBER TAXSIM model, in order to make after-tax comparisons with FECA benefits (which are not taxed). We could not calculate taxes for some annuitants; therefore, we assumed that these annuitants owed zero taxes. Enclosure II describes in more detail how we compared non-USPS FECA benefits to non-USPS retirement annuities.

To determine the experiences in states that limit workers' compensation benefits for workers at retirement age, we conducted case studies in four states that do so—Kentucky, Minnesota, Montana, and Tennessee. To identify the states, we first reviewed reports and interviewed officials from several organizations, including Workers Compensation Research Institute (WCRI); National Academy of Social Insurance; Workers' Injury Law & Advocacy Group; and National Council on Compensation Insurance. We analyzed WCRI's *Workers' Compensation Laws as of January 2010* (Cambridge, MA: October 2010) to identify states that limit benefits by retirement age but did not independently verify the information contained in this compilation. Of the eight states that, according to the WCRI review, limit workers' compensation benefits by age, we selected five states that limit workers' compensation benefits for workers at retirement age: Kentucky, Minnesota, Montana, North Dakota and Tennessee. We spoke with stakeholders in all of the states, except for North Dakota. We did not receive information from officials in North Dakota on their experiences within time frames that would have allowed us to include them in this report. In each of the four states, we interviewed workers' compensation board officials who manage and maintain state-level workers' compensation programs to discuss their experiences in administering workers' compensation benefits, particularly for older workers; and private sector attorneys who specialize in workers' compensation within their states to discuss their experiences handling cases involving older workers. We also reviewed specific elements of state law for the four selected states and, as appropriate, verified our analysis of state laws with cognizant state officials.

ENCLOSURE II. METHODOLOGICAL DETAILS ON THE COMPARISON OF FECA AND CSRS ANNUITY BENEFITS

Overview of the Matched Comparison Group Method

Comparing FECA benefits and retirement annuities requires us to estimate something that cannot be observed in the real world: the retirement benefits that FECA beneficiaries would have earned if they were never injured. We can observe either annuity or FECA payments at retirement age, depending on whether employees happened to be injured during their careers. In contrast, we cannot observe the counterfactual payment that the FECA beneficiaries would have received if they had not become sick or injured. The fact that employees become sick or injured prevents us from observing what they would have earned had they not become sick or injured. How do we estimate the counterfactual annuity incomes of FECA beneficiaries, given that we cannot observe them directly? One simple method would be to calculate the difference between annuity and FECA payments for retirement-age beneficiaries. If a typical beneficiary received more than a typical annuitant, one might conclude that structural features of the FECA program made those benefits more generous. The problem with the simple comparison is that it reflects characteristics of employees who are injured, in addition to characteristics of the FECA and CSRS annuity programs. An employee's work environment, long-term health, and attitudes toward risk could affect both income and the chance of receiving FECA benefits. FECA beneficiaries and annuitants may vary with respect to these characteristics when we observe them in 2010. For example, employees with physically demanding jobs, such as letter carriers and border patrol agents, may have higher risks of being injured and lower incomes than employees who work in less hazardous conditions and remain healthy enough to retire. FECA benefits might appear less generous, when, in fact, the difference is due to lower prior earnings among employees more prone to workplace injury. In a matched comparison group analysis, we compare FECA beneficiaries to annuitants who have similar incomes and potential to be injured on the job. By comparing FECA beneficiaries to annuitants with similar demographics, work environments, periods of employment, and incomes prior to injury or retirement, we can better isolate the difference in benefits due to program characteristics alone. If we match the groups on all characteristics that affect both income and the chance of becoming injured, statistical theory ensures that a simple comparison between groups can estimate the counterfactual annuity income that FECA beneficiaries would have earned.

Theory of the Matched Comparison Group Method

For all employees, let D_i equal 1 if the employees become eligible for FECA benefits and 0 otherwise. Let Y_{id} and Y_{ir} equal the employees' potential FECA and retirement annuity benefits that they could have earned if they were injured or worked to retirement, respectively. Because employees in the population of interest either get injured or remain healthy and retire, their observed benefits at retirement age equal

$$Y_i = D_i Y_{id} + (1 - D_i) Y_{ir} .$$

This makes clear that the observed benefits depend on both (1) whether the employees are injured (and the factors that lead to injury) and (2) the program features that determine Y_{id} and Y_{ir}. We need to estimate the expected difference between what FECA beneficiaries earn and what they would have earned in annuity benefits if they had not been injured. This is given by

$$j = E(Y_{id} - Y_{ir} | D_i = 1) = E(Y_{id} | D_i = 1) - E(Y_{ir} | D_i = 1) .$$

In statistics, this parameter is known as the Average Treatment Effect for the Treated. Here, the treatment effect of interest is the mean difference in retirement-age earnings in the potential states of injury and retirement, among those who were actually receiving FECA benefits in 2010. The key assumption required to estimate j from the observed earnings and group membership data is that D_i is independent of (Y_{id}, Y_{ir}), conditional on a vector of covariates X_i. In other words, FECA and annuity benefits are unrelated to the propensity to be injured among employees who have similar background characteristics. Using this assumption and the available data, causal inference theory ensures that $j = E(Y_i|X_i, D_i = 1) - E(Y_i|X_i, D_i = 0)$, which can be estimated from the observed data by replacing the random variables with their sample values and consistent estimators of sample means. We can estimate *j* using various methods, including statistical models that specify a functional form for $E(Y_i| Xi, D_i)$. In contrast, the matched comparison group method selects a sample of annuitants such that the empirical distributions of the covariates are as similar as possible to the covariate distributions for the FECA beneficiaries. Achieving this covariate balance conditions the comparison of sample means on X_i and estimates *j* without bias, assuming the treatment is unrelated to the potential outcomes among employees with the same characteristics (or "conditionally ignorable").[33]

Matching Methods

To construct the matched samples, we used a computer algorithm that selected the single closest annuitant for each FECA beneficiary, measured on the Mahalanobis measure of multivariate distance in X_i, and then returned each annuitant to the pool of potential matches after matching each FECA beneficiary. (This is known as one-to-one Mahalanobis matching with replacement.[34]) With about 75 annuitants available to match for each FECA beneficiary, we were able to combine exact matching and matching in distribution. Because occupation and agency may strongly affect work environment and income, we created one matched sample that was exactly matched on these variables. Exact matching potentially reduces the sample available to match on other variables, so we created a second sample that matched on the proportion of each group that had a "blue collar occupation," as defined by the Office of Personnel Management (OPM).[35] For all versions of the analysis, we assessed covariate balance using the sample moments and quantiles before and after matching. Although our data are not a probability sample, we calculated the standard error of the difference in mean benefits to assess the uncertainty of our estimates, using standard formulas for differences in means between independent samples. Our large sample sizes suggested that the estimated variances would have been small, regardless of the particular method used.

Population of Interest and Data Sources

We analyzed two populations of federal employees: those who were long-term, full-time FECA beneficiaries and at least 55 years old on June 30, 2010, and those who were CSRS annuitants on approximately the same date who were in the same age group. These individuals did not include those who received survivor benefits.[36] We assumed that the retirement age began at 55 years and limited our analysis to these subpopulations of both groups. We focused on this age group because 96 percent of annuitants in 2010 were at least 55 years old and because a younger group provides more data for analysis. In addition, 55 is the minimum age of retirement eligibility under CSRS.

The limited availability of historical data on federal employees also determined the population we analyzed. OPM's Central Personnel Data File (CPDF) was the primary source of data available on employment histories. The database contained information measured on the last day of each fiscal year since 1988. This period covered 54 percent of the people receiving long-term, full-time cash benefits in chargeback year 2010 who were at least 55 years old and who did not work for USPS. As a result, we could analyze only this subset of employees who worked after 1988.

The OPM personnel file provided relatively complete data on these employees. Data were available for an average of 63 percent of each employee's career, with 75 percent of employees having data for at least 71 percent of their careers.37 Data on the analysis variables were missing for only 0.4 to 1.8 percent of employees, depending on the variable. Although the limited scope of the OPM personnel data limits our analysis to employees working since 1988, this subset of people likely resembles current and future federal employees more closely than the employees we could not analyze.

We constructed the final data for analysis using the OPM personnel data, an administrative database on FECA beneficiaries from the Department of Labor (Labor), and an administrative database on annuitants from OPM. First, we selected from the Labor database the subset of FECA beneficiaries who worked for agencies other than USPS, were at least 55 years old in 2010, and received long-term, full-time cash benefits in chargeback year 2010 (14,983 people).[38]

We then selected all employees who received annuities and were at least 55 years old in 2010 from the OPM annuitant database (866,391 people). Finally, we matched the FECA beneficiaries and annuitants to their historical personnel data from OPM and kept for analysis only those employees working after 1988 who were covered by the CSRS retirement system.

The final dataset included approximately 301,000 annuitants and 4,000 FECA beneficiaries, depending on the variables required for analysis. These groups are smaller than the populations that Labor and OPM originally provided, due to our screening by age and retirement system and the lack of OPM personnel data for employees working prior to 1988.

Consequently, our results generalize only to the population of non-USPS, long-term, full-time FECA beneficiaries working after 1988 who were at least 55 years old in 2010.

Measurement of Characteristics for Matching Analysis

In this section, we describe the variables we used to conduct the analysis and our measurement of important concepts.

We measured most of the variables prior to the FECA beneficiary's last date of employment.[39]

This created a comparison group of annuitants with similar work histories prior to when the matched FECA beneficiary left federal employment.

- Benefits
  The benefit for FECA beneficiaries was their annual gross cash payments for chargeback year 2010, and the benefit for annuitants was their annual annuity income in fiscal year 2010. Using the TaxSim program developed by the National Bureau of Economic Research, we estimated the amount of taxes each annuitant might have paid on the gross benefit to create an after-tax measure.[40] Because FECA benefits are not subject to income tax, the adjustment helped ensure that we compared after-tax benefits for both groups. Due to missing and inconsistent data from OPM, we could not estimate taxes for 414 of the approximately 301,000 annuitants in our population of interest. We assumed that these annuitants owed zero taxes, which overestimated after-tax benefits. In addition, we assumed that each annuitant had a spouse older than the age of 65—the scenario for which taxes are lowest—because data on the annuitants' families were not available. These assumptions reduce any differences between after-tax annuities and FECA benefits for other otherwise equivalent employees.
- First year of federal employment
  We measured the first year of federal employment for both groups using the earliest service computation date for leave purposes in OPM's personnel data.

For employees who started after 1988, the earliest date likely equals their starting date because the personnel data would have covered their first year working and would not have reflected later adjustments due to lapses in service. For employees who started before 1988, the minimum date would equal the starting date for those workers who were employed continuously (at least 75 percent of workers in the OPM personnel data).

- Last year of federal employment
  We measured the last year of federal employment for both groups as the latest year in which the OPM personnel data recorded the employee as being on board.
- Length of service
  Our data allowed us to measure the length of service for FECA beneficiaries on (1) the date of injury, (2) the date of last employment, and (3) the date of entering the long-term, full-time benefit rolls. We chose to measure length of service as the time between the last year of employment and the maximum service computation date in OPM's personnel data. The maximum service computation date reflects adjustments for multiple spells of employment. Consequently, the time elapsed between the last year of employment and the service computation date should measure length of service at the time of separation.
  We calculated the same measure of length of service for annuitants, even though OPM provided the measure it used for calculating annuity benefits. For most employees, the OPM measure differed from the measure we calculated from OPM's personnel data by no more than 1.4 years, but we used our calculated measure to ensure that we measured length of service the same way for FECA beneficiaries and annuitants.
- Spells of employment
  We used OPM's personnel data to calculate the number of spells of employment from 1988 through 2010. Our measure underestimates the number of spells for employees who were working prior to 1988 and had more than one spell of employment. This error is likely to be slight, however, given that at least 75 percent of employees in OPM's personnel data after 1988 worked continuously. We controlled for number of spells to construct comparable work histories and to approximate an employee's risk preferences, assuming that having more spells is correlated with accepting more occupational risk.

- Prior income
  We measured income during each employee's career using salary data from OPM's personnel data. We measured the minimum, median, and maximum incomes for the employees' career for the portion of their career prior to the date of disability. (For annuitants, we measured income prior to their matched FECA beneficiaries' last years of employment.)
- Occupation, agency, education, and gender
  We used "occupation groups" defined by OPM to measure the type of work each employee performed. These groups included occupations that involved a similar type of work, such as the "engineering and architecture" group that included occupations involving "civil engineering" and "architecture."
  We used two-digit agency codes to identify the employing agency, such as the Departments of Commerce and Defense. For the FECA beneficiaries, we measured occupation and agency as close to the injury date as possible. For the annuitant group, we measured occupation and agency in the annuitants' last year of employment. Since occupation and agency do not change frequently over time, the exact timing of the measurements should not be consequential. We used OPM's personnel data file to determine gender and education for both groups of employees on the same dates as the measures of occupation and agency.

Balance of Characteristics before and after Matching

Table 4 and figure 4 describe the characteristics of the FECA beneficiaries and annuitants, prior to matching. As compared to the annuitants, the FECA beneficiaries stopped working at an earlier age, had fewer years of service, had lower prior incomes, were less educated, and were more likely to have an occupation defined by OPM as "blue-collar."

This suggests that the injured employees were more likely to have jobs that involved lower-paid physical labor. Despite these differences, the median FECA beneficiary earned 12.2 percent ($3,886) more in gross benefits than the median annuitant prior to matching.

Table 4. Characteristics of FECA Beneficiaries and Annuitants before Matching

	FECA beneficiaries				Annuitants			
	25th percentile	Median	Mean	75th percentile	25th percentile	Median	Mean	75th percentile
Outcome								
FECA cash benefits or CSRS annuity income in 2010 (nominal dollars)	$28,779	$35,638	$39,922	$46,634	$20,868	$31,752	$36,296	$47,472
FECA cash benefits or estimated after-tax CSRS annuity income in 2010 (nominal dollars)	$28,779	$35,638	$39,922	$46,634	$20,856	$30,570	$33,917	$43,932
Covariates								
First year of employment	1970	1974	1974	1978	1966	1970	1970	1975
Last year of employment	1990	1994	1995	1999	1993	1997	1998	2003
Age in 2010	60	65	66.4	72	63.1	68.7	69.5	75.3
Age in first year of employment	23.8	29	30.2	35.3	22.3	26.8	28.9	34.3
Age in last year of employment	46.1	51.3	51.5	56.8	53.7	56.5	56.9	60.6
Years of service[a]	15.6	21	21.1	26	23.6	28.7	27.9	32.5
Spells of employment	1	1	1	1	1	1	1	1
Minimum prior income (2011 dollars)	$38,409	$47,230	$50,655	$58,107	$39,331	$50,573	$55,398	$66,676
Median prior income (2011 dollars)	$41,248	$49,829	$54,191	$62,734	$42,772	$55,772	$60,617	$73,469
	FECA beneficiaries				Annuitants			

	25th percentile	Median	Mean	75th percentile	25th percentile	Median	Mean	75th percentile
Maximum prior income (2011 dollars)	$43,380	$52,738	$57,217	$66,555	$45,861	$61,047	$66,128	$81,356
No high school degree (percent)			20.6				13.3	
High school degree (percent)			35.4				32	
Some college (percent)			28				28.1	
College degree (percent)			8.9				13.8	
Graduate degree (percent)			6.9				12.8	
OPM blue-collar occupation (percent)			38.4				14.3	
Occupation group	Various				Various			
Agency	Various				Various			

Source: GAO analysis of Labor and OPM data.

Note: Populations include 4,006 FECA beneficiaries and 301,433 retired workers who were at least 55 years old in 2010, working after 1988, and covered by the CSRS retirement system. Some percentages do not total 100 percent, due to rounding.

[a] Length of service is the time between the last year of employment and the maximum service computation date in OPM's personnel data.

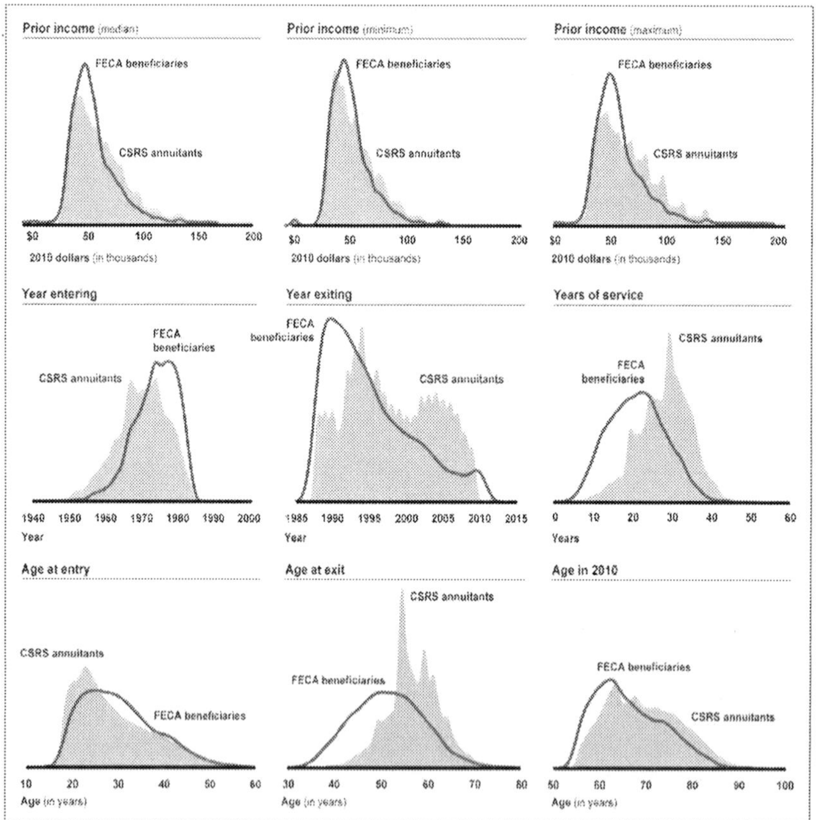

Source: GAO analysis of Labor and OPM data

Figure 4. Covariate Density Estimates for FECA Beneficiaries and Annuitants before Matching.

Our matching algorithm effectively corrected for these imbalances, as shown in table 5 and figure 5. The balance measures reflect the results of our analysis that used exact matching on occupation and agency.

All covariates are well-balanced in both the means and various quantiles. Other measures of the sample distribution of the covariates, such as the ratio of variances and mean differences between all empirical quantiles, showed similarly strong balance.

We achieved similar balance when we substituted an indicator for blue-collar occupation instead of exactly matching on occupation and agency.

Table 5. Characteristics of FECA Beneficiaries and Annuitants after Matching

	FECA beneficiaries				Retired			
	25th percentile	Median	Mean	75th percentile	25th percentile	Median	Mean	75th percentile
Outcome								
Before tax annuity or FECA cash benefits in 2010 (nominal dollars)	$28,853	$35,614	$39,946	$46,504	$20,409	$29,196	$33,813	$41,967
After-tax annuity or FECA cash benefits in 2010 (nominal dollars)	$28,853	$35,614	$39,946	$46,504	$20,400	$28,289	$31,775	$39,335
Covariates								
First year of employment	1970	1974	1974	1978	1970	1974	1973	1978
Age in 2010	61	65	66.5	72	61.1	65.3	66.6	71.7
Age in first year of employment	23.8	29	30.3	35.4	23.3	28.2	29.6	34.6
Age in last year of employment	45.9	51	51.2	56.3	45.6	50.8	50.8	55.8
Years of service[a]	15.6	20.8	20.9	25.6	16.3	21.2	21.2	26.1
Spells of employment	1	1	1	1	1	1	1	1
Minimum prior income (2011 dollars)	$38,466	$47,342	$50,784	$58,174	$39,235	$47,682	$50,924	$58,073
Median prior income (20,11 dollars)	$41,211	$49,803	$54,178	$62,710	$41,798	$50,026	$54,113	$62,319
Maximum prior income (2011 dollars)	$43,277	$52,511	$57,016	$66,384	$43,873	$52,513	$57,275	$66,944
No high school degree (percent)			20.7				20.2	
High school degree (percent)			35.5				36.5	
Some college (percent)			27.9				27.9	
College degree (percent)			9				8.6	
Graduate degree (percent)			6.9				6.9	
Occupation group			Same				Same	
Agency			Same				Same	

Source: GAO analysis of Labor and OPM data. Note: Populations include 3,864 disabled and 3,864 matched retired workers who were at least 55 years old in 2010, working after 1988, and covered by the CSRS retirement system. The number of disabled workers excludes 142 who could not be matched. After-tax estimates assume that taxpayers had a spouse older than 65. Some percentages do not total 100 percent, due to rounding.

[a] Years of service were based on the amount of time between the employees' earliest date of service and the FECA beneficiaries' date of injury.

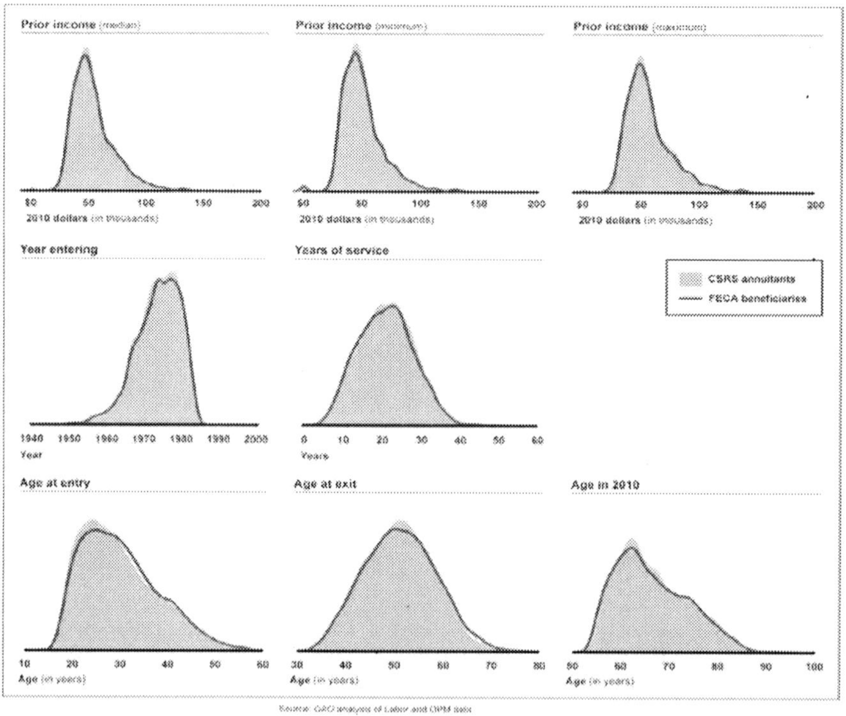

Figure 5. Covariate Density Estimates for FECA Beneficiaries and Annuitants after Matching.

We found results similar to those in table 6 of enclosure III using samples matched on the proportion of each group having a blue-collar occupation instead of exactly matched on occupation and agency. Using this alternative matched sample, the median before-tax estimates of the difference in benefits for all FECA beneficiaries varied by no more than 1 percent from the estimates we produced using the matched sample described above.

ENCLOSURE III. DIFFERENCE IN BENEFITS BETWEEN NON-USPS FECA BENEFICIARIES AND MATCHED RETIRED EMPLOYEES

Entries are the difference in FECA beneficiaries versus matched annuitant benefits, using the retirement comparison and exact matching on occupation and agency. After-tax estimates assume that the taxpayer had a spouse of the same age.

For additional technical information on methodology in comparing FECA benefits to retirement annuities, refer to enclosure II.

Table 6. Differences in Benefits between Non-USPS FECA Beneficiaries and Matched Retired Employees

	Dollars (2010)				Proportional difference between FECA benefit and annuity (percent)			
	Before taxes		After taxes		Before taxes		After taxes	
Group	Median	Mean	Median	Mean	Median	Mean	Median	Mean
Overall	6,418	6,133	7,324	8,172	22	18.1	25.9	25.7
Years of service[a]								
Less than 10	12,450	9,352	12,450	10,071	74.1	44.6	74.1	49.8
10 to 19	9,685	8,219	9,956	9,494	41.7	29.9	43.4	36.2
20 to 29	6,059	5,603	7,296	8,013	18.8	15	23.5	22.9
30 or more	912	740	3,692	4,619	2.1	1.6	9.2	10.6
Years since exit[b]								
Less than 4	5,675	7,297	7,781	10,525	14.8	17	21.5	26.5
4 to 7	6,237	5,705	7,941	8,351	18.1	14.6	24.3	22.9
8 to 11	12,280	11,003	13,010	12,971	44.8	32.7	48.7	40.9
12 or more	13,030	12,652	13,145	13,702	60.9	49.5	61.8	55.9
Maximum prior income								
1st quartile	6,295	6,006	6,325	6,358	33.6	30.4	33.9	32.8
2nd quartile	7,315	7,060	7,772	7,841	29.5	27.4	31.9	31.3
3rd quartile	5,990	6,195	7,412	7,930	18	18.3	23.3	24.6
4th quartile	4,031	6,157	8,686	11,377	7.6	11.1	17.9	22.7
Age in 2010								
55 to 59	2,015	1,823	3,632	4,702	5.8	4.7	11	13
60 to 64	4,409	4,211	5,781	6,623	13.6	11.5	18.7	19.3
65 to 69	6,693	6,286	7,682	8,238	22.7	18.3	27	25.4
70 and older	11,159	10,834	11,337	12,041	49.2	39.8	50.4	46.2

Source: GAO analysis of Labor and OPM data.

[a] Years of service were based on the amount of time between the employees' earliest date of service and the FECA beneficiaries' date of injury.

[b] Years since exit measures the time elapsed between the employees' last year of federal employment and 2010.

Enclosure IV. Characteristics of (1) All FECA Beneficiaries, (2) Long-Term, Full-Time FECA Beneficiaries, and (3) Long-Term, Full-Time Retirement-Age FECA Beneficiaries for 2010[41]

All FECA Beneficiaries

Table 7. Distribution of Benefit Type for All FECA Beneficiaries (2010)

	All		USPS		Non-USPS	
	Number of FECA beneficiaries	Percent	Number of FECA beneficiaries	Percent	Number of FECA beneficiaries	Percent
Medical benefits only	109,913	35.8%	52,891	40.5%	57,022	32.3%
Long-term, full-time	31,880	10.4%	12,349	9.5%	19,531	11.1%
Part-time	10,594	3.5%	2,501	1.9%	8,093	4.6%
Short-term	24,549	8.0%	15,567	11.9%	8,982	5.1%
Schedule award	7,596	2.5%	3,816	2.9%	3,780	2.1%
Survivor benefits	4,642	1.5%	625	0.5%	4,017	2.3%
Closed case	108,495	35.4%	39,398	30.2%	69,097	39.2%
Other	9,236	3.0%	3,336	2.6%	5,900	3.3%
Total	**306,905**	**100.0%**	**130,483**	**100.0%**	**176,422**	**100.0%**

Source: GAO analysis of Labor data.

Note: Other includes administrative reviewed, reopened, case retired or awaiting retirement, claim under development, claim unreviewed, claim destroyed, and claims with overpayments.

Table 8. Distribution of Age for All FECA Beneficiaries (2010)

	All		USPS		Non-USPS	
	Number of FECA beneficiaries	Percent	Number of FECA beneficiaries	Percent	Number of FECA beneficiaries	Percent
Less than 20	1,404	0.5%	29	0.0%	1,375	0.8%
20-29	20,548	6.7%	3,273	2.5%	17,275	9.8%
30-39	39,194	12.8%	13,933	10.7%	25,261	14.3%
40-49	70,829	23.1%	35,883	27.5%	34,946	19.8%
50-59	102,336	33.3%	53,143	40.7%	49,193	27.9%
60-64	36,076	11.8%	15,556	11.9%	20,520	11.6%
65 and older	36,333	11.8%	8,655	6.6%	27,678	15.7%
Missing, not applicable	185	0.1%	11	0.0%	174	0.1%
Total	**306,905**	**100.0%**	**130,483**	**100.0%**	**176,422**	**100.0%**
Median Age	52 years		52 years		52 years	

Source: GAO analysis of Labor data.

Table 9. Distribution of Gender for All FECA Beneficiaries (2010)

	All		USPS		Non-USPS	
	Number of FECA beneficiaries	Percent	Number of FECA beneficiaries	Percent	Number of FECA beneficiaries	Percent
Male	171,927	56.1%	62,745	48.1%	109,182	62.1%
Female	134,311	43.9%	67,696	51.9%	66,615	37.9%
Total	**306,238**	**100.0%**	**130,441**	**100.0%**	**175,797**	**100.0%**

Source: GAO analysis of Labor data.

Note: Total excludes 667 cases where gender was missing.

Table 10. Years from Date of Injury to 2010 for All FECA Beneficiaries

	All		USPS		Non-USPS	
	Number of FECA beneficiaries	Percent	Number of FECA beneficiaries	Percent	Number of FECA beneficiaries	Percent
Less than 1 year ago	114,321	37.2%	42,880	32.9%	71,441	40.5%
1 to 5 years ago	104,829	34.2%	51,174	39.2%	53,655	30.4%
6 to 10 years ago	30,779	10.0%	17,985	13.8%	12,794	7.3%
11 to 20 years ago	29,182	9.5%	12,599	9.7%	16,583	9.4%
21 to 30 years ago	16,012	5.2%	3,514	2.7%	12,498	7.1%
31 to 40 years ago	9,244	3.0%	1,910	1.5%	7,334	4.2%
41 or more years ago	2,538	0.8%	421	0.3%	2,117	1.2%
Total	**306,905**	**100.0%**	**130,483**	**100.0%**	**176,422**	**100.0%**

Source: GAO analysis of Labor data.

Table 11. Distribution of Annual Cash Benefits for All FECA Beneficiaries (2010)

	All		USPS		Non-USPS	
	Number of FECA beneficiaries	Percent	Number of FECA beneficiaries	Percent	Number of FECA beneficiaries	Percent
$0	221,522	73.4%	93,555	73.4%	127,967	73.4%
$1 - $9,999	23,368	7.7%	12,268	9.6%	11,100	6.4%
$10,000 - $19,999	14,519	4.8%	6,206	4.9%	8,313	4.8%
$20,000 - $29,999	15,394	5.1%	4,741	3.7%	10,653	6.1%
$30,000 - $39,999	16,160	5.4%	8,386	6.6%	7,774	4.5%
$40,000 - $49,999	5,558	1.8%	1,654	1.3%	3,904	2.2%
$50,000 - $59,999	2,172	0.7%	265	0.2%	1,907	1.1%
$60,000 - $69,999	1,252	0.4%	138	0.1%	1,114	0.6%
$70,000 - $79,999	681	0.2%	62	0.0%	619	0.4%
$80,000 - $89,999	386	0.1%	35	0.0%	351	0.2%
$90,000 - $99,999	407	0.1%	25	0.0%	382	0.2%
$100,000 or more	407	0.1%	88	0.1%	319	0.2%
Total	**301,826**	**100.0%**	**127,423**	**100.0%**	**174,403**	**100.0%**
Median benefit (excluding $0)	$21,504		$17,371		$23,574	

Source: GAO analysis of Labor data.

Note: Table excludes cases where benefits were less than zero. Amounts less than zero are due to accounting for, for example, chargebacks to the claim for overpayments.

Table 12. Distribution of Annual Medical Benefits for All FECA Beneficiaries (2010)

	All		USPS		Non-USPS	
	Number of FECA beneficiaries	Percent	Number of FECA beneficiaries	Percent	Number of FECA beneficiaries	Percent
$0	79,305	26.0%	23,071	17.8%	56,234	32.1%
$1 - $9,999	203,493	66.7%	95,254	73.4%	108,239	61.7%
$10,000 - $19,999	13,715	4.5%	6,998	5.4%	6,717	3.8%
$20,000 - $29,999	4,228	1.4%	2,136	1.6%	2,092	1.2%
$30,000 - $39,999	1,793	0.6%	929	0.7%	864	0.5%
$40,000 - $49,999	907	0.3%	457	0.4%	450	0.3%
$50,000 - $59,999	532	0.2%	273	0.2%	259	0.1%
$60,000 - $69,999	349	0.1%	175	0.1%	174	0.1%
$70,000 - $79,999	189	0.1%	90	0.1%	99	0.1%
$80,000 - $89,999	158	0.1%	79	0.1%	79	0.0%
$90,000 - $99,999	99	0.0%	53	0.0%	46	0.0%
$100,000 or more	386	0.1%	185	0.1%	201	0.1%
Total	**305,154**	**100.0%**	**129,700**	**100.0%**	**175,454**	**100.0%**
Median benefit (excluding $0)	$888		$975		$823	

Source: GAO analysis of Labor data.

Note: Table excludes cases where benefits were less than zero. Amounts less than zero are due to accounting for, for example, chargebacks to the claim for overpayments.

Table 13. Distribution of Total Annual Benefits (Cash and Medical Benefits Combined) for All FECA Beneficiaries (2010)

	All		USPS		Non-USPS	
	Number of FECA beneficiaries	Percent	Number of FECA beneficiaries	Percent	Number of FECA beneficiaries	Percent
$0	56,688	18.8%	17,064	13.4%	39,624	22.8%
$1 - $9,999	173,538	57.6%	81,301	63.8%	92,237	53.1%
$10,000 - $19,999	19,117	6.3%	8,547	6.7%	10,570	6.1%
$20,000 - $29,999	16,079	5.3%	5,685	4.5%	10,394	6.0%
$30,000 - $39,999	14,921	5.0%	6,661	5.2%	8,260	4.8%
$40,000 - $49,999	9,044	3.0%	4,098	3.2%	4,946	2.8%
$50,000 - $59,999	4,615	1.5%	1,766	1.4%	2,849	1.6%
$60,000 - $69,999	2,637	0.9%	854	0.7%	1,783	1.0%
$70,000 - $79,999	1,511	0.5%	437	0.3%	1,074	0.6%
$80,000 - $89,999	926	0.3%	290	0.2%	636	0.4%
$90,000 - $99,999	691	0.2%	182	0.1%	509	0.3%
$100,000 or more	1,411	0.5%	475	0.4%	936	0.5%
Total	**301,178**	**100.0%**	**127,360**	**100.0%**	**173,818**	**100.0%**
Median benefit (excluding $0)	$1,563		$1,463		$1,707	

Source: GAO analysis of Labor data.

Note: Table excludes cases where benefits were less than zero. Amounts less than zero are due to accounting for, for example, chargebacks to the claim for overpayments.

Long-Term, Full-Time FECA Beneficiaries[42]

Table 14. Distribution of Long-Term, Full-Time Beneficiaries (2010)

	All		USPS		Non-USPS	
	Number of long-term, full-time beneficiaries	Percent	Number of long-term, full-time beneficiaries	Percent	Number of long-term, full-time beneficiaries	Percent
Long term, full-time	31,880	100.0%	12,349	38.7%	19,531	61.3%

Source: GAO analysis of Labor data.

Table 15. Distribution of Age of Long-Term, Full-Time Beneficiaries (2010)

	All		USPS		Non-USPS	
	Number of long-term, full-time beneficiaries	Percent	Number of long-term, full-time beneficiaries	Percent	Number of long-term, full-time beneficiaries	Percent
Less than 20	7	0.0%	0	0.0%	7	0.0%
20-29	187	0.6%	64	0.5%	123	0.6%
30-39	1,090	3.4%	591	4.8%	499	2.6%
40-49	4,299	13.5%	2,474	20.0%	1,825	9.3%
50-59	9,544	29.9%	4,871	39.4%	4,673	23.9%
60-64	5,147	16.1%	1,876	15.2%	3,271	16.7%
65 and older	11,606	36.4%	2,473	20.0%	9,133	46.8%
Total	**31,880**	**100.0%**	**12,349**	**100.0%**	**19,531**	**100.0%**
Median age	60 years		56 years		63 years	

Source: GAO analysis of Labor data.

Table 16. Distribution of Gender of Long-Term, Full-Time Beneficiaries (2010)

	All		USPS		Non-USPS	
	Number of long-term, full-time beneficiaries	Percent	Number of long-term, full-time beneficiaries	Percent	Number of long-term, full-time beneficiaries	Percent
Male	17,705	55.5%	5,554	45.0%	12,151	62.2%
Female	14,174	44.5%	6,795	55.0%	7,379	37.8%
Total	31,879	100.0%	12,349	100.0%	19,530	100.0%

Source: GAO analysis of Labor data.

Note: Table excludes cases where gender was missing.

Table 17. Years from Date of Injury to 2010 for Long-Term, Full-Time Beneficiaries

	All		USPS		Non-USPS	
	Number of long-term, full-time beneficiaries	Percent	Number of long-term, full-time beneficiaries	Percent	Number of long-term, full-time beneficiaries	Percent
Less than 1 year ago	1,110	3.48%	674	5.46%	436	2.23%
1 year ago	1,437	4.51%	923	7.47%	514	2.63%
2 years ago	1,171	3.67%	711	5.76%	460	2.36%
3 years ago	1,131	3.55%	613	4.96%	518	2.65%
4 years ago	1,053	3.30%	605	4.90%	448	2.29%
5 years ago	1,107	3.47%	575	4.66%	532	2.72%
6 years ago	1,106	3.47%	580	4.70%	526	2.69%
7 years ago	1,144	3.59%	585	4.74%	559	2.86%
8 years ago	1,019	3.20%	564	4.57%	455	2.33%
9 years ago	1,040	3.26%	569	4.61%	471	2.41%
10 years ago	1,042	3.27%	540	4.37%	502	2.57%
11-15 years ago	4,072	12.77%	1,716	13.90%	2,536	12.06%
16-20 years ago	4,126	12.94%	1,212	9.81%	2,914	14.92%
21-25 years ago	3,870	12.14%	867	7.02%	3,003	15.38%
26-30 years ago	2,731	8.57%	486	3.94%	2,245	11.49%
31-35 years ago	2,497	7.83%	571	4.62%	1,926	9.86%
36-40 years ago	1,396	4.38%	351	2.84%	1,045	5.35%
41 or more years ago	828	2.60%	207	1.68%	621	3.18%
Total	**31,880**		**12,349**		**19,531**	

Source: GAO analysis of Labor data.

Note: Some percentages do not total 100 percent, due to rounding.

Table 18. Distribution of Annual Cash Benefits for Long-Term, Full-Time Beneficiaries (2010)

	All		USPS		Non-USPS	
	Number of long-term, full-time beneficiaries	Percent	Number of long-term, full-time beneficiaries	Percent	Number of long-term, full-time beneficiaries	Percent
$0	163	0.5%	70	0.6%	93	0.5%
$1 - $9,999	1,096	3.4%	691	5.6%	405	2.1%
$10,000 - $19,999	3,161	9.9%	1,170	9.5%	1,991	10.2%
$20,000 - $29,999	7,558	23.7%	1,812	14.7%	5,746	29.5%
$30,000 - $39,999	12,391	38.9%	6,899	56.0%	5,492	28.2%
$40,000 - $49,999	4,029	12.7%	1,339	10.9%	2,690	13.8%
$50,000 - $59,999	1,411	4.4%	159	1.3%	1,252	6.4%
$60,000 - $69,999	848	2.7%	83	0.7%	765	3.9%
$70,000 - $79,999	501	1.6%	36	0.3%	465	2.4%
$80,000 - $89,999	261	0.8%	16	0.1%	245	1.3%
$90,000 - $99,999	298	0.9%	10	0.1%	288	1.5%
$100,000 or more	116	0.4%	39	0.3%	77	0.4%
Total	**31,833**	**100.0%**	**12,324**	**100.0%**	**19,509**	**100.0%**
Median benefit (excluding $0)	$33,554		$34,459		$32,492	

Source: GAO analysis of Labor data.

Note: Table excludes cases where benefits were less than zero. Amounts less than zero are due to accounting for, for example, chargebacks to the claim for overpayments.

Table 19. Distribution of Annual Medical Benefits for Long-Term, Full-Time Beneficiaries (2010)

	All		USPS		Non-USPS	
	Number of long-term, full-time beneficiaries	Percent	Number of long-term, full-time beneficiaries	Percent	Number of long-term, full-time beneficiaries	Percent
$0	6,946	21.8%	1,555	12.6%	5,391	27.6%
$1 - $9,999	17,026	53.5%	6,931	56.2%	10,095	51.8%
$10,000 - $19,999	4,177	13.1%	2,053	16.6%	2,124	10.9%
$20,000 - $29,999	1,551	4.9%	747	6.1%	804	4.1%
$30,000 - $39,999	754	2.4%	377	3.1%	377	1.9%
$40,000 - $49,999	452	1.4%	225	1.8%	227	1.2%
$50,000 - $59,999	272	0.9%	133	1.1%	139	0.7%
$60,000 - $69,999	188	0.6%	95	0.8%	93	0.5%
$70,000 - $79,999	105	0.3%	49	0.4%	56	0.3%
$80,000 - $89,999	83	0.3%	37	0.3%	46	0.2%
$90,000 - $99,999	57	0.2%	29	0.2%	28	0.1%
$100,000 or more	228	0.7%	105	0.9%	123	0.6%
Total	31,839	100.0%	12,336	100.0%	19,503	100.0%
Median benefit (excluding $0)	$4,931		$6,056		$4,016	

Source: GAO analysis of Labor data.

Note: Table excludes cases where benefits were less than zero.

Amounts less than zero are due to accounting for, for example, chargebacks to the claim for overpayments.

Table 20. Distribution of Total Annual Benefits (Cash and Medical Benefits Combined) for Long-Term, Full-Time Beneficiaries (2010)

	All		USPS		Non-USPS	
	Number of long-term, full-time beneficiaries	Percent	Number of long-term, full-time beneficiaries	Percent	Number of long-term, full-time beneficiaries	Percent
$0	11	0.0%	2	0.0%	9	0.0%
$1 - $9,999	639	2.0%	352	2.9%	287	1.5%
$10,000 - $19,999	2,067	6.5%	749	6.1%	1,318	6.8%
$20,000 - $29,999	5,507	17.3%	1,237	10.0%	4,270	21.9%
$30,000 - $39,999	9,366	29.4%	4,241	34.4%	5,125	26.3%
$40,000 - $49,999	6,207	19.5%	2,993	24.3%	3,214	16.5%
$50,000 - $59,999	3,124	9.8%	1,248	10.1%	1,876	9.6%
$60,000 - $69,999	1,794	5.6%	582	4.7%	1,212	6.2%
$70,000 - $79,999	1,136	3.6%	323	2.6%	813	4.2%
$80,000 - $89,999	647	2.0%	189	1.5%	458	2.3%
$90,000 - $99,999	475	1.5%	116	0.9%	359	1.8%
$100,000 or more	870	2.7%	300	2.4%	570	2.9%
Total	**31,843**	**100.0%**	**12,332**	**100.0%**	**19,511**	**100.0%**
Median benefit (excluding $0)	$38,282		$39,177		$37,289	

Source: GAO analysis of Labor data.

Note: Table excludes cases where benefits were less than zero. Amounts less than zero are due to accounting for, for example, chargebacks to the claim for overpayments.

Retirement-Age Beneficiaries on Long-Term, Full-Time Rolls[43]

Table 21. Distribution of Retirement-Age Beneficiaries on Long-Term, Full-Time Rolls (2010)

	All		USPS		Non-USPS	
	Number of retirement-age beneficiaries	Percent	Number of retirement-age beneficiaries	Percent	Number of retirement-age beneficiaries	Percent
Long term, full-time	10,873	100.0%	2,286	21.0%	8,587	79.0%

Source: GAO analysis of Labor data.

Table 22. Distribution of Gender of Retirement-Age Beneficiaries on Long-Term, Full-Time Rolls (2010)

	All		USPS		Non-USPS	
	Number of retirement-age beneficiaries	Percent	Number of retirement-age beneficiaries	Percent	Number of retirement-age beneficiaries	Percent
Male	7,200	66.2%	1,472	64.4%	5,728	66.7%
Female	3,673	33.8%	814	35.6%	2,859	33.3%
Total	**10,873**	**100.0%**	**2,286**	**100.0%**	**8,587**	**100.0%**

Source: GAO analysis of Labor data.

Note: Table excludes case where gender was missing.

Table 23. Years from Date of Injury to 2010 for Retirement-age Beneficiaries on Long-Term, Full-Time Rolls (2010)

	All		USPS		Non-USPS	
	Number of retirement-age beneficiaries	Percent	Number of retirement-age beneficiaries	Percent	Number of retirement-age beneficiaries	Percent
Less than 1 year ago	28	0.26%	11	0.48%	17	0.20%
1 year ago	30	0.28%	13	0.57%	17	0.20%
2 years ago	37	0.34%	16	0.70%	21	0.24%
3 years ago	39	0.36%	19	0.83%	20	0.23%
4 years ago	44	0.40%	13	0.57%	31	0.36%
5 years ago	64	0.59%	20	0.87%	44	0.51%
6 years ago	72	0.66%	32	1.40%	40	0.47%
7 years ago	88	0.81%	27	1.18%	61	0.71%
8 years ago	82	0.75%	20	0.87%	62	0.72%
9 years ago	109	1.00%	43	1.88%	66	0.77%
10 years ago	118	1.09%	36	1.57%	82	0.95%
11-15 years ago	703	6.47%	193	8.44%	510	5.94%
16-20 years ago	1,424	13.10%	240	10.50%	1,184	13.79%
21-25 years ago	1,973	18.15%	306	13.39%	1,667	19.41%
26-30 years ago	1,843	16.95%	298	13.04%	1,545	17.99%
31-35 years ago	2,126	19.55%	475	20.78%	1,651	19.23%
36-40 years ago	1,289	11.86%	320	14.00%	969	11.28%
41 or more years ago	804	7.39%	204	8.92%	600	6.99%
Total	**10,873**		**2,286**		**8,587**	

Source: GAO analysis of Labor data.

Note: Some percentages do not total 100 percent, due to rounding.

End Notes

[1] Codified at 5 U.S.C.§ 8101 et seq.

[2] Cash benefits are paid for lost wages, loss of, or loss of use of, a body part or function (schedule awards), and death of an employee as a result of a workplace injury (survivor benefits). Schedule awards and survivor benefits can be in addition to any benefits payable for lost wages. The total for cash benefits includes amounts for long-term, full-time benefits; short-term benefits; part-time benefits; schedule awards; and survivor benefits.

[3] USPS employees are not included in OPM's Central Personnel Data File (CPDF) because USPS does not report personnel data to OPM.

[4] For example, we needed a service computation date to determine the length of service for annuitants. However, the service computation data we received from USPS for the period 1988 to 2010 was missing these data for 16 to 90 percent of employees, depending on the year.

[5] FECA benefits are paid out of the Employees' Compensation Fund, and most are charged back to the employees' agency. Labor's chargeback year for FECA agency billing purposes ends June 30.

[6] The age at which an individual can receive full retirement benefits under the Social Security Act (known as the "full retirement age" or the "normal retirement age," or NRA) ranges from 65 to 67, depending on the individual's year of birth. For those born in 1937 and earlier, NRA is 65; for those born in years 1943-1954, the NRA is 66; for those born in 1960 and later, the NRA is 67; for years of birth in between those just cited, the NRA is interpolated by 2 months per year of birth. See http://www.ssa.gov/oact/progdata/nra.html .

[7] We included only FECA recipients who were covered by CSRS because the majority of annuitants currently receiving annuities are covered by CSRS. According to OPM, approximately 81 percent of fiscal year 2010 employee annuitants were CSRS annuitants.

[8] We used the National Bureau of Economic Research's (NBER) TAXSIM to determine federal and state income taxes for annuitants. TAXSIM is NBER's FORTRAN program for calculating liabilities under U.S. federal and state income tax laws from individual data. The TAXSIM Model (http://www.nber.org/taxsim) simulates the U.S. federal and state income tax rules. See Daniel Richard Feenberg and Elizabeth Coutts, "An Introduction to the TAXSIM Model," *Journal of Policy Analysis and Management*, vol. 12, no. 1(winter, 1993), 189-194.

[9] In general, part-time benefits are determined by calculating the difference between the employee's preinjury and postinjury monthly wages.

[10] USPS receives no annual appropriations for purposes other than revenue forgone on free and reduced rate mail. USPS generates revenue through the sale of postage and postal-related products and services and borrows money from the U.S. Treasury via the Federal Financing Bank. It has relied increasingly on this debt to fund its operations. According to USPS, it paid $1.3 billion for workers' compensation costs in 2010.

[11] Employees eligible for FECA benefits could also be eligible for retirement disability benefits from OPM or Social Security Disability Insurance benefits. Depending on which benefits employees are entitled to, employees might have to make an election between them. In many cases in which individuals receive benefits from different programs simultaneously, one benefit would likely be offset against the other to some extent.

[12] Under both CSRS and FERS, the date of employees' eligibility to retire with an annuity depends on their age and years of service. The amount of the retirement annuity is determined by three factors: the number of years of service, the accrual rate at which benefits are earned for each year of service, and the salary base to which the accrual rate is applied. In both CSRS and FERS, the salary base is the average of the highest 3 consecutive years of basic pay. This is often called "high-3" pay. Under both systems, a worker with at

least 30 years of service can retire at the age of 55 (for FERS, this is true if the worker was born before 1948).

[13] All federal employees who are enrolled in FERS pay Social Security taxes and earn Social Security benefits. Federal employees enrolled in either CSRS or FERS also may contribute to the federal 401(k)-like program, the Thrift Savings Plan (TSP); however, only employees enrolled in FERS are eligible for employer matching contributions to the TSP.

[14] GAO, *Federal Workers' Compensation: Questions to Consider in Changing Benefits for Older Beneficiaries*, GAO-11-854T (Washington, D.C.: July 26, 2011); and *Federal Employees' Compensation Act: Issues Associated With Changing Benefits for Older Beneficiaries*, GAO/GGD-96-138BR (Washington, D.C.: Aug. 14, 1996).

[15] A federal employee or surviving dependent is not entitled to sue the United States or recover damages for such injury or death under any other law for a work injury.

[16] In 2010, of the 79,261 people who received cash benefits, 24,549 received short-term benefits, 10,594 received part-time benefits, 7,596 received schedule awards, and 4,642 received survivor benefits.

[17] This group of long-term, full-time beneficiaries does not include those individuals receiving part-time benefits, schedule awards, and survivor benefits.

[18] Because of the way Labor maintains its data, it is not possible to know whether an individual whose case closed in 2010 did or did not receive cash benefits. Cases may be closed for various reasons, including re-employment or because an individual has recovered from their work-related injury.

[19] Our method of analysis ensured that only those who had reached full Social Security retirement age in 2010 were included in this calculation. About 11 percent (32,563 of 306,905) of all FECA beneficiaries are eligible for full retirement under the Social Security Act.

[20] Of all FECA beneficiaries, 407 received $100,000 or more in cash benefits in 2010. According to Labor, this can occur if a beneficiary received lump sum schedule award payments, retroactive claims payments, or payments provided for by special legislation.

[21] The available historical data on federal employees limited our analysis to those who (a) were non-USPS, and (b) had electronic records in the OPM current employee database between 1988 and 2010.

[22] This analysis only included cash benefits for long-term, full-time beneficiaries, who are considered unable to work in any capacity, for 2010. This analysis does not include closed cases, claims with medical payments only, FECA beneficiaries who received survivor benefits, or schedule awards. The analysis also does not distinguish between FECA beneficiaries who have no dependents, and received 66-2/3 percent of their preinjury salaries and those beneficiaries with dependents who received 75 percent of their preinjury salaries. Further, this analysis does not include individuals receiving part- time Loss of Wage Earning Capacity (LWEC) benefits. In general, part-time benefits are determined by calculating the difference between the employee's preinjury and postinjury monthly wage. These individuals do not receive full disability benefits from FECA, because it has been determined that they are capable of working part-time or with restrictions.

[23] Unlike FECA benefits, a portion of each CSRS retiree's annuity is taxed. Because OPM uses complex formulas to determine the taxed portion of the annuity, we estimated federal and state income taxes using the National Bureau of Economic Research's (NBER) TAXSIM program. TAXSIM is NBER's program for calculating liabilities under U.S. federal and state income tax laws from individual data. The TAXSIM Model (http://www.nber.org/ taxsim) simulates the U.S. federal and state income tax rules. See Daniel Richard Feenberg and Elizabeth Coutts, "An Introduction to the TAXSIM Model," Journal of Policy Analysis and Management, vol. 12, no. 1 (winter, 1993), 189-194. We could not estimate taxes for a number of annuitants; therefore, in our tax analyses, we assumed these annuitants owed zero taxes.

[24] Our analysis showed that 71 percent of FECA beneficiaries had higher benefits than their retiree counterparts before taxes; 77 percent had higher benefits after adjusting for taxes.

Given the trend shown here, the remaining 29 percent of FECA beneficiaries (23 percent after taxes) whose benefits were lower than their retiree counterparts' annuities most likely were injured later in their careers and after many years of service.

[25] This is an annual adjustment of FECA benefits based on changes in the Consumer Price Index.

[26] According to the Workers' Compensation Research Institute (WCRI) review of state workers' compensation laws as of January 2010, eight states limit workers' compensation benefits by age. We initially selected five of those states—Kentucky, Minnesota, Montana, North Dakota, and Tennessee—that limit workers' compensation benefits for workers at retirement age, according to WCRI. We did not receive information from officials in North Dakota on their experiences within time frames that would have allowed us to include them in this report. There are other states that limit workers' compensation benefits based on an age other than retirement age. For example, Florida limits workers' compensation benefits at age 75, according to the WCRI review. See Ramona Tanabe, *Workers' Compensation Laws as of January 2010*, WCRI (Cambridge, MA: October 2010).

[27] Injured workers with a permanent total disability continue to receive medical care benefits after reaching retirement age under the workers' compensation program in all four states, according to workers' compensation officials. Montana defines permanent total disability as a condition that prevents a return to regular employment, which means work on a recurring basis, according to a workers' compensation official.

[28] However, Kentucky allows workers with a permanent total disability to receive wage-loss benefits from the state for up to 2 years after the employees' last injury, so workers in Kentucky may in some instances continue receiving wage-loss benefits after reaching retirement age.

[29] Although most employees are covered by Social Security, federal law generally allows states to enter into voluntary agreements to provide Social Security coverage to certain state and local government employees. In the four states we reviewed, the percentage of state and local government workers covered by Social Security ranged from about 75 percent to 94 percent in 2007, according to prior GAO work. See GAO, *Social Security Administration: Management Oversight Needed to Ensure Accurate Treatment of State and Local Government Employees*, GAO-10-938 (Washington, D.C.: Oct. 4, 2010).

[30] Legislative Audit Division, State of Montana, *Financial Audit for the Fiscal Year Ended June 30, 2005, Montana State Fund* (Helena, MT: October 2005).

[31] FECA benefits are paid out of the Employees' Compensation Fund, and most are charged back to the employees' agency. Labor's chargeback year for FECA agency billing purposes ends June 30, 2010.

[32] A service computation date is a date that is used to determine benefits and is generally based on how long the person has been in the federal service.

[33] Matching allows us to control for the propensity to get injured on the job without making assumptions about the functional form of the relationships among Y_i, X_i, and D_i. We use this nonparametric method of adjusting for the covariates, instead of parametric models, because we lack substantial prior knowledge on how federal employees become injured.

[34] We matched directly on X_i, rather than on an estimate of the propensity score, $E(D_i \mid X_i)$. This avoided making potentially inaccurate assumptions about the functional form relating employees' characteristics to their chance of being injured.

[35] Examples of blue-collar occupations include aircraft electrician, roofer, and forklift operator.

[36] This analysis does not distinguish between FECA beneficiaries who have no dependents, and received 66-2/3 percent of their preinjury salaries and those beneficiaries with dependents who received 75 percent of their preinjury salaries.

[37] We measured coverage rates using the ratio of the length of time an employee was observed in the CPDF to the time elapsed between the minimum service computation year and the final year of employment observed in the CPDF.

[38] FECA benefits are paid out of the Employees' Compensation Fund and most are charged back to the employees' agency. Labor's chargeback year for FECA agency billing purposes ends June 30, 2010.

[39] To do this, we created subsets of the FECA beneficiaries according to their final year of federal employment and then found matched annuitants with similar covariates measured up to this year. We combined the year-specific samples to create an overall matched sample.

[40] Daniel Richard Feenberg and Elizabeth Coutts, "An Introduction to the TAXSIM Model," *Journal of Policy Analysis and Management*, vol. 12, no 1 (winter 1993), 189-194. Accessed via the Internet on Nov. 30, 2011, at http://www.nber.org/~taxsim/taxsim-calc9 index.html.

[41] All data presented in this enclosure are from chargeback year 2010. See enclosure I for more information on the source of the data.

[42] This group of long-term, full-time beneficiaries does not include those individuals receiving part-time benefits, schedule awards, and survivor benefits.

[43] Includes only those FECA beneficiaries on the long-term, full-time rolls who were of full retirement age as set forth in the Social Security Act.

In: The Federal Employees' Compensation Act ISBN: 978-1-62081-729-2
Editors: A. K. James and F. E. Davis

Chapter 3

FEDERAL EMPLOYEES' COMPENSATION ACT: PRELIMINARY OBSERVATIONS ON FRAUD-PREVENTION CONTROLS*

United States Government Accountability Office

January 25, 2012

Congressional Committees

According to the Department of Labor (Labor), in fiscal year 2010 about 251,000 federal and postal employees and their survivors received wage-loss compensation, medical and vocational rehabilitation services, and death benefits through the Federal Employees' Compensation Act (FECA) program. Administered by Labor, the FECA program provides benefits to federal employees who sustained injuries or illnesses while performing their federal duties. Employees must submit claims to their employing agency, which are then reviewed by Labor. For those claims that are approved, employing agencies reimburse Labor for payments made to their employees, while Labor bears most of the program's administrative costs. Wage-loss benefits for eligible workers—including those who are at, or older than, retirement age—with total disabilities are generally 66.67 percent of the worker's salary (with

---

* This is an edited, reformatted and augmented version of the GAO-12-402 Report to Congressional Committees, dated January, 2012.

no spouse or dependent) or 75 percent for a worker with a spouse or dependent. FECA wage-loss compensation benefits are tax free and not subject to time or age limits.

Labor's Office of Workers' Compensation Programs (OWCP) estimated that future actuarial liabilities for governmentwide FECA compensation payments to those receiving benefits as of fiscal year 2011 would total nearly $30 billion (this amount does not include any costs for workers added to the FECA rolls in future years). In 2010, the United States Postal Service (USPS) Inspector General (IG) reported that USPS alone had more than $12 billion of the $30 billion in estimated actuarial FECA liabilities. In April 2011, the USPS IG testified that USPS had removed 476 claimants from the program based on disability fraud since October 2008 and recovered more than $83 million in judgments. Given the significant projected outlays of the governmentwide FECA program and prior USPS IG findings of fraud, you asked us to provide preliminary observations on our ongoing work examining FECA fraud-prevention controls and discuss related prior work conducted by us and other federal agencies. We will continue to review the identified issues and report more fully on our findings at a later date.

To provide these preliminary observations on governmentwide FECA fraud-prevention controls, we reviewed Labor's annual performance and accountability reports, the FECA procedures manual and internal controls, OWCP's accountability reviews, relevant agencies' Office of Inspector General reports, and applicable laws and regulations. We interviewed officials at OWCP headquarters and officials responsible for managing the FECA program at six federal agencies that employ FECA claimants: USPS, United States Navy (Navy), Department of Veterans Affairs (VA), United States Army (Army), Department of Homeland Security (DHS), and United States Air Force (Air Force). We selected these employing agencies because they had the highest total amount of FECA expenditures in fiscal year 2010 among federal agencies. Combined, these employing agencies represent 73 percent of total FECA program future liabilities as of September 30, 2011. Because these employing agencies are not representative of the entire FECA program, our findings cannot be generalized beyond these six agencies. This report's findings are primarily based on document reviews and discussions with agency officials. As such, we have not validated whether controls discussed in this report are actually being consistently followed or are effective. On November 9, 2011, we issued a statement for the record to the Senate Committee on Homeland Security and Governmental Affairs detailing our preliminary observations on FECA fraud prevention controls.[1] We also discussed our key findings with agency officials and incorporated their comments into the statement where appropriate. Those findings and comments are included in this report.

We conducted this portion of our ongoing performance audit from June 2011 through January 2012, in accordance with generally accepted government auditing standards. Those standards require that we plan and perform the audit to obtain sufficient, appropriate evidence to provide a reasonable basis for our findings and conclusions based on our audit objectives. We believe that the evidence obtained provides a reasonable basis for our findings and conclusions based on our audit objectives.

RESULTS IN BRIEF

Our work to this point has identified several promising practices that could help to reduce the risk of fraud within the FECA program. The promising practices link back to fraud-prevention concepts contained in GAO's Fraud Prevention Framework and Standards for Internal Control in the Federal Government,[2] and include agencies' use of full-time staff dedicated to the FECA program, periodic reviews of claimants' continued eligibility, data analysis for potential fraud indicators, and effective use of investigative resources. These promising practices have already resulted in successful investigations and prosecutions of FECA-related fraud at some agencies, and could help to further enhance the program's fraud-prevention controls. However, our preliminary work has also identified several potential vulnerabilities in the program's design and controls that could increase the risk for fraud. Specifically, we found that limited access to necessary data is potentially reducing agencies' ability to effectively monitor claims and wage-loss information. In addition, agencies' reliance on self-reported data related to wages and dependent status, lack of a physician selected by the government throughout the process, and difficulties associated with successful investigations and prosecutions all potentially reduce the program's ability to prevent and detect fraudulent activity. Labor and employing agencies generally agreed with the preliminary findings presented in this report and provided technical comments, which were incorporated into this report. We plan to follow up on the promising practices and potential vulnerabilities as part of our ongoing work, although our progress has been slowed by difficulties in accessing certain databases.

BACKGROUND

The FECA program covers over 2.7 million civilian federal and postal employees in more than 70 agencies, providing wage-loss compensation and payments for medical treatment to employees injured while performing their federal duties.[3] FECA claims are initially received at the employing agency, then forwarded to Labor's OWCP where eligibility and payment decisions are made. Every year, employing agencies reimburse OWCP for the amounts paid to their employees in FECA compensation during the previous year. Certain government corporations and USPS also make payments to Labor for program administrative fees.[4] Figure 1 displays the standard process for FECA claims reviews and payments by OWCP.

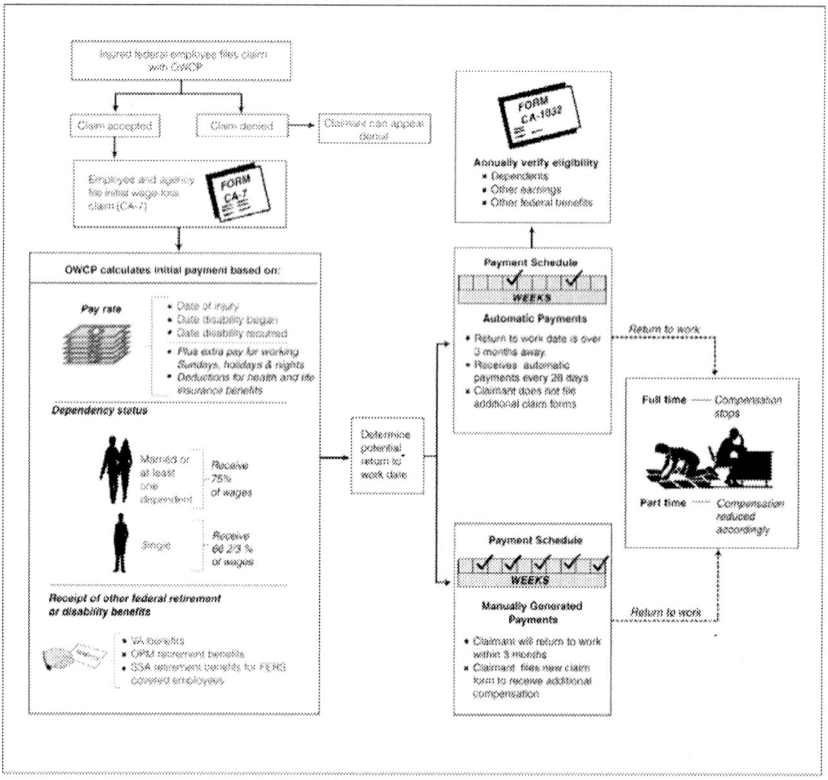

Source: GAO analysis; images, Art Explosion.

Figure 1. FECA Claims Process.

OWCP is the central point where FECA claims are processed and eligibility and benefit decisions are made. Claims examiners at OWCP's 12 FECA district offices determine applicants' eligibility for FECA benefits and process claims for wage-loss payments. FECA laws and regulations specify complex criteria for computing compensation payments. Using information provided by the employing agency and the claimant on a claims form, OWCP calculates compensation based on a number of factors, including the claimant's rate of pay, the claimant's marital status, and whether or not the claimant has dependents. In addition, claimants cannot receive FECA benefits at the same time they receive certain other federal disability or retirement benefits, or must have benefits reduced to eliminate duplicate payments. For example, Social Security Administration (SSA) disability benefits are reduced if an individual is also receiving FECA payments.

According to OWCP officials, initial claims received from employing agencies are reviewed to assess the existence of key elements. The elements include evidence that the claim was filed within FECA's statutory time requirements, that the employee was, at the time of injury, disease, or death, an employee of the United States, and that the employee was injured while on duty, and that the condition resulted from the work-related injury. If the key elements are in place, OWCP will approve a claim and begin processing reimbursements for medical costs. After initial claim approval, additional reviews are done while a claim remains active if the claim exceeds certain dollar thresholds. Once a claim is approved, payments are sent directly to the claimant or provider. An employee can continue to receive compensation for as long as medical evidence shows that the employee is totally or partially disabled and that the disability is related to the accepted injury or condition. OWCP considers claimants who are not expected to return to work within 3 months to be on its periodic rolls for payment purposes.[5] OWCP officials review medical evidence annually for claimants on total disability receiving long-term compensation who are on the program's periodic rolls, and every 3 years for claimants on the periodic rolls who have been determined to not have any wage-earning capacity. Claimants are also required to submit an annual form (CA-1032) stating whether their income or dependent status has changed. The form must be signed to acknowledge evidence of benefit eligibility and to acknowledge that criminal prosecution may result if deliberate falsehood is provided. If questions arise about medical evidence submitted by the claimant, OWCP can request a second medical examination be performed by a physician of its choosing.

Observations from Preliminary Work Identify Promising Practices and Potential Vulnerabilities

Our preliminary observations indicate that employing agencies and Labor have instituted some promising practices that may help reduce fraudulent FECA claims, yet potential vulnerabilities continue to exist. We plan to determine the effect of these practices in our future work. GAO's Framework for Fraud Prevention, Detection, and Prosecution, developed during previous program audits, emphasizes that comprehensive controls are necessary to minimize fraud, waste, and abuse within any federal program, including FECA.[6] GAO's Standards for Internal Control in the Federal Government[7] also outlines key control practices that are integral parts of an effective control environment. The promising practices and potential vulnerabilities below relate to issues raised in these guidelines.

Promising Practices

We have identified several promising practices that employing agencies and Labor have implemented that may help to reduce fraudulent FECA claims. We are planning to look further into these practices as part of our ongoing work.

Dedicated Full-Time Staff

Three employing agencies informed us that they employed dedicated, full-time FECA program staff including injury compensation specialists and other staff, which, according to officials, helps staff gain program knowledge and expertise. It also allows program staff to specialize in FECA claims and reviews without having to perform additional duties. Agencies with full time staff may be able to dedicate resources to training them in fraud prevention, which is a positive practice noted in GAO's fraud-prevention framework. GAO's Standards for Internal Control in the Federal Government[8] also specifically mentions that appropriate, competent personnel are a key element to an effective control environment. Officials from one employing agency with this structure stated that having dedicated and experienced FECA staff allows them to conduct more aggressive monitoring of long-term workers' compensation cases. Labor officials agreed that agencies that can devote dedicated full time resources are positioned better to manage the program. Examples include the following:

- FECA staff in one Navy region reported having an average of 15 years of program experience, which they said helps them to identify specific indicators of potential fraud.
- According to the Air Force, it has specific teams that specialize in reviewing FECA claims at different phases of the claims process.
- USPS officials also stated they assign staff full time to manage FECA cases.

In addition, in 2008, we recommended that the Secretary of Labor direct OWCP to take steps to focus attention on the recovery of FECA overpayments, such as determining whether having fiscal staff dedicated to recovering overpayments would increase its recovery.[9] Labor stated that it carefully evaluated having fiscal staff dedicated to recovering overpayments. However, given the integral involvement of claims examiners in overpayment processing, the unavailability of fiscal staff to undertake this specialized activity, and expected continued budget constraints, Labor believes that keeping this function with claims examiners is the most cost-effective debt-collection strategy.

Periodic Reviews

Officials at five employing agencies and Labor have instituted periodic reviews of active FECA claims, which may improve overall program controls. Specifically, several agencies reported that annual reviews of FECA case files were used to help increase program officials' awareness of potential fraudulent activities.

These controls fall within the detection and monitoring component of GAO's fraud-prevention framework and could help to validate claimants' stated medical conditions, income information, and dependent information. GAO's Standards for Internal Control in the Federal Government also states that monitoring activities, such as comparisons of different data sets to one another, can help to encourage continued compliance with applicable laws and regulations.

Agency officials stated that these types of reviews assist with identifying claimants who are not eligible to continue to receive FECA benefits. According to agency staff:

- Labor requires long-term claimants to submit updated claim documentation about wages earned and dependent status for annual reviews. While much of the information provided on the CA-1032 is self-reported, the requirement for annual submissions can help identify necessary changes to benefits. In addition, Labor officials stated they also perform regular medical-claim reviews depending on the status of a case.
- Staff at one Navy regional office send annual questionnaires to claimants to determine if information, including income and dependent status, is consistent with annual documentation submitted to Labor.
- A DHS component agency sends periodic letters to claimants asking about their current status. If DHS determines that action should be taken, DHS then sends a letter to Labor requesting the claim be closed.
- Under DOD policies, Air Force, Army, and Navy staff are required to conduct an annual review of selected long-term claim files and medical documentation to determine whether claimants are receiving compensation benefits they are entitled to and identify claimants who are fit to return to work.
- The Air Force has developed quarterly working groups to review all paid compensation benefits.
- USPS performs periodic reviews of claimant data. USPS IG officials identified a claimant who fraudulently claimed $190,000 in mileage reimbursements for travel to therapy almost every day for 5 years, including weekends and holidays.[10]

Data Analysis

Officials from employing agencies and Labor stated that their program staff conducted data analysis, such as comparisons of mileage claims to medical bills, to verify information submitted by claimants. Agencies also reported using available data sources to verify whether claimants should continue to receive FECA benefits. Similar to the periodic reviews previously discussed, these controls fall within the monitoring component of GAO's fraud-prevention framework and could help to validate claimants' self-reported income and medical-condition information. Data sources reviewed ranged from federal agency data to other publicly available information. Agencies also conduct reviews of claimant physician and prescription drug payments to identify fraud. Specifically, according to agency officials:

- Labor gives each employing agency access to its Agency Query System (AQS), which allows agencies to electronically review information on FECA claims, including current claims status, wage-compensation payment details, and medical-reimbursement details.
- Labor officials also stated they provide at least quarterly, and for some employing agencies weekly, extracts from their data system that give employing agencies information on wage-compensation payments, medical-billing payments, and case-management data.
- The Navy reviews pharmacy bills, medical-diagnosis codes, and mileage-reimbursement details from the AQS system on a case-by-case basis to determine whether physician claims are related to the injury sustained by the claimant and to identify whether mileage for physician visits was reimbursed on days when the claimant did not visit a physician.
- Navy officials use publicly available state government information to identify claimants who owned and received income from their own businesses. For example, one public records search found that a FECA claimant was an active owner of a gentleman's club while he was fraudulently receiving FECA wage-loss benefits.
- Officials from employing agencies and Labor stated that they reviewed SSA's Death Master File periodically to identify benefits erroneously dispersed to deceased individuals' survivors. Specifically, Labor said it conducts monthly data matches with SSA's Death Master File records and plans to revise the forms used in survivors' claims to gather Social Security numbers for survivors and beneficiaries, enabling Labor to match all FECA payees with SSA death records.
- VA has developed a process that allows the agency to track prescription drug usage claims and identify anomalies.

Agency Utilization of Investigative Resources and Prosecutions

Four employing agencies reported that using investigative resources by investigating potential fraud cases helped to increase program controls. The Navy FECA component has assigned responsibilities to staff that investigate and help prosecute fraudulent FECA claims, while the Air Force has designated staff that refers allegations to its Office of Special Investigations. USPS program officials reported that they refer potential fraud cases internally to USPS IG officials for investigation and prosecution. The investigation and effective prosecution of claimants fraudulently receiving benefits is a key element in GAO's fraud-prevention framework. While these activities are often the most costly and least effective means of reducing fraud in a program, the deterrent value of prosecuting those who commit fraud sends the message that fraudulent claims will not be tolerated. Examples of the effective integration of investigative resources provided by these employing agencies include the following:

- The Air Force discussed its plan to hire staff in early fiscal year 2012 to conduct background investigations and surveillance of claimants to determine whether they are entitled to receive FECA benefits.
- The USPS IG reported that since October 2008 it identified and facilitated terminating benefits for 476 claimants who were committing workers' compensation fraud, and recovered over $83 million in medical and disability judgments.
- Navy officials stated that their internal investigators' work at one region led to 10 convictions from 2007 to 2011 and an $8.6 million cost-avoidance to the agency.
    - One individual received monthly workers' compensation payments after falsely denying that he had outside employment and outside income while claiming total disability that prevented him from working. Interviews with former employers uncovered that this claimant had been employed and been paid over $100,000 per year while he was receiving benefits. This individual was sentenced to 18 months in prison, 3 years supervised probation, and $302,380 in restitution for making a false statement to obtain FECA benefits.
    - Another individual collected FECA benefits made out to his father for 4 years after his father was deceased. This individual was sentenced to 5 years of probation and full restitution in the amount of $53,410.
- DHS officials within the Transportation Security Administration stated they have successfully used an internal affairs unit consisting of seven staff members to examine and respond to fraud, waste, and abuse cases and make referrals to investigators. The investigators then conduct video surveillance and examine data to find potential fraud.
- A recent Labor IG testimony cited numerous Labor IG investigations that have been conducted over the years focusing on FECA claimants who work while continuing to receive benefits, and on medical or other service providers who bill the program for services not rendered.

Potential Vulnerabilities

Our preliminary observations also identified potential vulnerabilities in the FECA program fraud-prevention controls that could increase the risk of claimants receiving benefits they are not entitled to. Again, we plan to examine these potential vulnerabilities as part of our ongoing work.

Limited Access to Data

We found that management of the FECA program could be affected by limited access to necessary data. Specifically, agency officials stated the program lacked proper coordination among federal agencies and that there was limited or no access to data sources that could help reduce duplicate payments. For example, Labor does not have authority to compare private or public wage data with FECA wage-loss compensation information to identify potential fraud. This prevents agencies from verifying key eligibility criteria submitted by claimants, such as income. GAO's fraud-prevention framework emphasizes effective monitoring of continued compliance with program guidelines, and outlines how validating information with external data can assist with this process. Specific potential vulnerabilities identified in the area included the following:

- Program officials at Labor and the employing agencies do not have access to payroll information included in the National Directory of New Hires (NDNH) and federal employee payroll data, which could help reduce duplicate payments by identifying unreported income.[11] In a previous report, we recommended that Labor develop a proposal seeking legislative authority to enter into a data-matching agreement with the Department of Health and Human Services (HHS) to identify FECA claimants who have earnings reported in the NDNH.[12] However, Labor officials stated that they investigated using NDNH and communicated with HHS, but determined that this would not be an effective solution due to cost issues, limited participation by employers in the NDNH, and the likelihood that illegitimate earnings would not be listed. As an alternative, Labor recently provided testimony proposing legislative reforms to FECA that would enhance its ability to assist FECA beneficiaries. As part of this reform, OWCP sought authority to match Social Security wage data with FECA files. OWCP currently is required to ask each individual recipient to sign a voluntary release to obtain such wage information. According to

Labor, direct authority would allow automated screening to assess whether claimants are receiving salary, pay, or remuneration prohibited by the statute or receiving an inappropriately high level of benefits. It would be important to assess whether access to Social Security wage data is an effective alternative to access to NDNH data, and we plan to assess this as part of our ongoing work.

- Navy and Air Force officials cited difficulty coordinating with VA to determine whether individuals are receiving disability benefits for the same conditions related to FECA claims. This information is key for employing agencies to assess whether claimants received duplicate benefits for the same injuries under both VA disability benefits and FECA benefits. VA commented that privacy concerns related to providing beneficiary data to external agencies has affected coordination.
- An employing agency official stated that Labor does not provide them with remote access to the claimant's annual certification form CA-1032, which would be useful for their periodic review efforts. However, Labor does allow employing agency officials to view the CA-1032 forms if the officials come to a Labor district office. The CA-1032 form contains information on a claimant's income and dependent status, which is useful when employing agencies review claims files for continued eligibility. We raise this issue because, as stated above, the Navy utilizes information submitted to Labor as part of its periodic review efforts.
- A 2010 SSA IG audit found individuals receiving duplicate benefits for SSA and FECA. According to the SSA IG, development of a computer-matching agreement with Labor and its FECA payments database would allow SSA to reduce the number of duplicate SSA payments by verifying the accuracy of payment eligibility. According to the SSA IG report, the agreement has not been finalized with Labor due to changes in personnel at SSA.

Reliance on Self-Reported Data

Our preliminary observations identified program processes that relied heavily on data self-reported by claimants that is not always verified by agency officials. Not verifying information concerning wages earned and dependent status reported by claimants creates potential vulnerabilities within the program. For example, individuals who are working can self-certify that they have no other income, and continue to remain on the program while their statements are not verified. Prior reports by us and Labor's IG have shown that relying on claimant-reported data could lead to overpayments. For example:

- A 2008 GAO report found that Labor relied on unverified, self-reported information from claimants that was not always timely or correct.[13] Specifically, the annual CA-1032 forms submitted to Labor to determine whether a beneficiary is entitled to continue receiving benefits relies on statements made by the claimant that are not verified.
- A 2007 Labor IG report also found that an OWCP district office did not consistently ensure that claimants returned their annual form CA-1032 or adjust benefits when the information reported by claimants indicated a change in their eligibility.[14] Labor agreed with the findings of this report.
- During fiscal year 2004, claimants and beneficiaries continued to receive compensation payments even though they had not provided required timely evidence of continuing eligibility.
- In one case, the claimant's augmented payment rate was not reduced even though the claimant reported that his spouse was no longer a dependent.

According to Labor officials, a new case-management system was deployed after the Labor IG audit field work was conducted, which addresses some of the issues raised in the Labor IG report.

Physicians Selected by the Government Not Present at Key Control Points

Our preliminary observations found that FECA program regulations allow claimants to select their own physician, and also requires examination by a physician employed or selected by the government only when a second opinion is deemed necessary by the government. We found this could result in essential processes within the FECA program operating without reviews by physicians selected by the government. This potential vulnerability affects key control processes outlined in GAO's fraud-prevention framework in two areas: first, the lack of reviews when assessing validity of initial claims and second, the lack of the same when monitoring the duration of the injury. However, the addition of a government physician into the process does not necessarily mitigate all risks, and costs associated with additional medical reviews would need to be considered. For example, there may be difficulties in successfully obtaining information from physicians representing the government's interest. Specifically, a prior GAO report found challenges in obtaining sound or thorough evidence from physicians approved by Labor in Black Lung Benefits Program claims for miners.[15] Our report also noted that physicians stated that guidance provided by Labor for effectively and completely documenting their medical opinions was not clear, which resulted in the challenges in providing useful information to Labor concerning Black Lung claims. Details of this potential vulnerability include the following:

- Labor, not the claimant's employing agency, determines if a second opinion is necessary. Employing-agency officials, including officials from DHS and USPS stated that there have been instances where Labor failed to respond to their requests to have a second-opinion examination performed at the employing agencies' request even though the costs would be borne by their agencies. We did not verify these claims. Labor officials stated that its claims examiners are trained to review files and make the appropriate case-management decision on the need for a second opinion. In addition, they stated that resources associated with second opinions include significant time and effort for a claims examiner to review a file, document the need for a second opinion, and determine the specific issues to be reviewed by the physician. Finally, Labor officials noted that numerous requests by employing agencies for second opinions can put a strain on the limited number of physician staff it uses for these examinations.

Difficulties Associated with Investigations and Prosecutions

Officials at multiple employing agencies covered in our work to date stated that they faced difficulties successfully investigating and prosecuting fraud. GAO's fraud-prevention framework states that targeted investigations and prosecutions, though costly and resource intensive, can help deter future fraud and ultimately save money. We plan to follow up with agency IG and United States Attorney officials to gain their perspective on FECA fraud cases as part of our ongoing work. Details offered by employing-agency program officials included the following:

- Officials at DOD stated that their investigative units do not normally invest resources in FECA fraud cases because national defense, antiterrorism, and violent crimes cases are higher priorities.

- USPS officials also stated that, in their experience, limited resources at United States Attorneys offices means that those attorneys will often not prosecute cases with an alleged fraud of less than $100,000. According to these officials, many of their strong allegations of fraud and abuse fall below this amount when estimating the cost of fraud that has already occurred.
- In addition to the challenges noted above related to fraud investigations, in 2008, we recommended that OWCP take steps to focus attention on recovering FECA overpayments. Specifically, we recommended considering reducing the dollar threshold for waiving overpayments as OWCP's overpayment processing data system develops additional capabilities. With respect to reducing the waiver threshold, Labor declined to consider reducing the dollar threshold while their current processing data system was developing additional capabilities to recover overpayments.

GAO's Plans to Further Assess Controls and Perform Data Analysis as Part of Ongoing Work

We plan to follow up on these promising practices and potential weaknesses as part of our ongoing review of FECA fraud-prevention controls. We will also determine whether duplication of benefits and other problems within the FECA program may have contributed to specific cases of fraud and abuse or other program vulnerabilities and develop illustrative case studies as appropriate. To complete this work, we have attempted to obtain access to NDNH data. However, HHS has denied access to the NDNH database because they assert that we do not have authority to obtain NDNH data, despite the fact that we have a broad right of access to all federal agency records.[16] HHS' denial of access has slowed the progress of this engagement reviewing federal beneficiary fraud and abuse and has limited our ability to assess the potential vulnerability of the FECA program to fraud and abuse at a national level. Although we have been able to obtain some of the data from a number of states, we have not received complete data from all states contacted. Legislation that is currently pending in the House and Senate (H.R. 2146, S. 237) would refute HHS' erroneous interpretation of our statutory access rights and would ensure that we have access to the NDNH and can complete our congressionally requested work in a timely manner.

In addition to our fraud-prevention work in the FECA program, we are conducting two other program-related engagements. Those engagements focus largely on issues related to retirement-age FECA beneficiaries. The results of that work will also be reported separately.

AGENCY COMMENTS AND OUR EVALUATION

On November 9, 2011, we issued a statement for the record to the Senate Committee on Homeland Security and Governmental Affairs detailing our preliminary observations on FECA fraud prevention controls.[17] At that time, we discussed our key findings with Labor and officials at the six employing agencies. Labor and the employing agencies generally agreed with the preliminary findings and provided technical comments, which were incorporated into the statement. Those findings and associated technical comments are included in this report.

Gregory D. Kutz
Director
Forensic Audits and Investigative Service

End Notes

[1] GAO, *Federal Employees' Compensation Act: Preliminary Observations on Fraud-Prevention Controls*, GAO-12-212T (Washington, D.C.: Nov. 9, 2011).

[2] GAO, *Hurricanes Katrina and Rita Disaster Relief: Prevention Is Key to Minimizing Fraud, Waste, and Abuse in Recovery Efforts*, GAO-07-418T (Washington, D.C.: Jan. 29, 2007); and *Internal Control: Standards for Internal Control in the Federal Government*, GAO/AIMD-00-21.3.1 (Washington, D.C.: November 1999).

[3] 5 U.S.C. §8101, et seq.

[4] Mixed-ownership government corporations such as the Federal Deposit Insurance Corporation are required to provide additional funds to cover their share of the costs of administering the program for their employees. See 5 U.S.C. §8147(c).

[5] Employees on the periodic rolls have total disabilities or injuries that have lasted or are expected to last for prolonged periods.

[6] GAO.

[7] GAO.

[8] GAO.

[9] GAO, *Federal Workers' Compensation: Better Data and Management Strategies Would Strengthen Efforts to Prevent and Address Improper Payments*, GAO-08-284 (Washington, D.C.: Feb. 26, 2008).

[10] United States Postal Service, Office of the Inspector General, *Postal Service Workers' Compensation Program Audit Report*, HR-AR-11-007 (Washington, D.C.: Sept 30, 2011).

[11] NDNH is a national directory of employment information that contains, among other data, quarterly wage data on individual employees and is maintained by the Department of Health and Human Services (HHS).

[12] GAO.

[13] GAO.

[14] U.S. Department of Labor, Office of Inspector General -Office of Audit, *Mechanisms Used to Identify Changes in Eligibility Are Inadequate at the FECA District Office in Jacksonville, Florida*, 04-07-004-04-431 (Washington, D.C.: Sept. 28, 2007).

[15] GAO, *Black Lung Benefits Program: Administrative and Structural Changes Could Improve Miners' Ability to Pursue Claims,* GAO-10-7 (Washington, D.C.: Oct. 30, 2009).

[16] 31 U.S.C. § 716(a).

[17] GAO.

In: The Federal Employees' Compensation Act ISBN: 978-1-62081-729-2
Editors: A. K. James and F. E. Davis

Chapter 4

STATEMENT OF CHRISTINE M. GRIFFIN. HEARING ON "EXAMINING THE FEDERAL WORKERS' COMPENSATION PROGRAM FOR INJURED EMPLOYEES"*

Chairman Akaka, Ranking Member Johnson, and members of the Subcommittee:

Thank you for the opportunity to testify today regarding the Office of Personnel Management's (OPM's) views on retirement issues related to legislative reform proposals to the Federal Employees Compensation Act (FECA).

Administered by the Department of Labor's Office of Workers' Compensation Programs (OWCP), FECA is a robust program that provides workers' compensation coverage to approximately 2.8 million federal civilian employees, including those in the U.S. Postal Service.

I will defer to the Department of Labor (DOL) to provide a more comprehensive overview of the various FECA reform proposals.

However, I look forward to discussing OPM's support of a workers' compensation system that is equitable to employers and employees, concerns with retirement changes under FECA reform proposals, and efforts to improve opportunities for federal employment of individuals with disabilities.

---

* This is an edited, reformatted and augmented version of the remarks given on July 26, 2011 before the Senate Committee on Homeland Security and Governmental Affairs.

PROPOSALS TO REFORM FECA

The current workers' compensation system provides a reasonable benefit comparable to an employee's income when they were able to work. When an employee reaches retirement age, however, the FECA benefits in many instances are more generous compared to what the employee would receive as a retiree. While retirement eligible employees under FECA have the right to elect coverage under their retirement plan, there is little incentive to do so because the workers' compensation benefits far exceed those benefits available under employees' retirement plans. The average federal employee voluntarily retiring under the Civil Service Retirement System (CSRS) receives an annuity of about 60 percent of their "high-three" average salary, most of which is taxable, compared to a tax free 75 percent or 66.66 percent FECA benefit. Therefore, the vast majority of long-term FECA claimants remain on the FECA rolls well past retirement age.

To address the retirement equity issue under FECA, the DOL and Senator Susan Collins have offered two different reform proposals. The President's budget request for fiscal year 2012 proposes reforms to the current FECA program that would standardize FECA benefits, allow for a retirement conversion benefit, and result in cost savings. The proposal from DOL would reduce a retirement eligible FECA claimant's benefits to 50 percent of their gross salary at date of injury (with cost of living adjustments), a level closer to what their retirement benefit would have been after a career of service This concept has the advantage of simplicity and uniformity of coverage. Regardless of an individual's particular retirement system, the claimant would be treated fairly and equitably upon reaching retirement age. In addition, FECA claimants would not change coverage systems from workers' compensation to one of the retirement programs. The President's budget estimates the FECA reform proposal would have Government-wide savings of more than $400,000,000 over ten years.

Legislation introduced by Senator Collins, S. 261, the Federal Employees' Compensation Reform Act, would take retirement eligible individuals off the compensation rolls and place them onto retirement rolls. We have strong concerns with the approach taken by S. 261, which we have detailed below, and believe that the approach offered by the DOL proposal represents a more fair and equitable treatment under FECA reform.

The House Education and the Workforce Committee recently approved a bipartisan FECA reform bill, H.R. 2465, which incorporates portions of the

Administration's FECA proposal, but does not affect issues with retirement. As such, we will not comment on the legislation at this time.

COMMENTS ON S. 261, THE FEDERAL EMPLOYEES' COMPENSATION REFORM ACT

S. 261 would require a system change, and at Social Security retirement age, FECA benefits would terminate if the individual were eligible for a CSRS or Federal Employee Retirement System (FERS) annuity. The bill, however, makes no provision for any other retirement changes.

Employees and employers do not make retirement contributions, including into Social Security or the Thrift Savings Plan (TSP) for those employees enrolled in FERS, while an employee is receiving workers compensation benefits. While the conversion concept would deal with all individuals receiving compensation regardless of their retirement system, S. 261 would only apply to employees covered by CSRS and FERS. However, while CSRS and FERS do cover the majority of federal employees, there are numerous retirement systems that cover federal employees such as the Foreign Service or Federal Reserve. To fully cover all individuals, the system change concept would require that these retirement plans be amended. As drafted, S. 261 would provide for retirement based only upon employment performed before an employee's injury. This could result in many individuals being placed in extreme financial hardship with a very small annuity and without health benefits. While differences would depend upon circumstances, it would be plausible that a $4,000 per month beneficiary could be converted to a $300 per month annuitant with no health benefits. Another possibly unintended and inequitable consequence is that individuals with the least amount of service at the time of their injuries and who would not meet annuity requirements would not be subject to S. 261 and therefore would receive much higher benefits than injured employees with more service. Even though individuals who concurrently apply for FECA benefits and FERS disability benefits will have their FERS benefit recomputed at age 62 with added service credit and an enhanced average salary, such individuals will still suffer from the loss of Social Security and their TSP for the period of disability. It would be possible to amend S. 261 to equitably provide for individuals subject to change from the workers' compensation program to a retirement system, but to do so would be very complicated. Presumably, equity would require that a system change benefit yield a retirement benefit comparable to what the individual would have received had their employment not been prematurely interrupted by an injury or illness. This would require a formula for adjusting service credit and annual salary. Furthermore, since FERS is only one tier of a three-tier retirement plan, addressing the loss of Social Security and TSP for the compensation period would also be necessary. Additionally, each federal retirement system that covers individuals under FECA would have to be individually modified based upon its particular benefit provisions. While the conversion concept would require only minimal administrative resources for implementation, each and every retirement system would require major changes utilizing substantial resources under the system change concept.

Improving Workers Compensation and Employment for People with Disabilities

OPM supports improving workers compensation for employees that have been injured during their employment, and the agency strongly supports efforts to improve employment for people with disabilities. One year ago today, President Obama signed Executive Order (E.O.) 13548 to Increase Federal Employment of Individuals with Disabilities. In February, I testified about OPM's efforts to improve federal employment of people with disabilities. OPM continues to partner with agencies across the federal government, including DOL's OWCP, to provide comprehensive training for federal agencies on: the E.O.; model recruitment strategies; reasonable accommodation policies and procedures; the Department of Defense's program to provide free accommodations to all federal employees with disabilities; and DOL's return to work strategies. Agencies are making strides toward the President's goal of hiring 100,000 people with disabilities over the next five years. They are beginning aggressive efforts to tap into the tremendous talents of people with disabilities, a long neglected segment of our society with a lot to offer the federal government.

Conclusion

OPM supports the Administration's efforts to reform FECA in an equitable and fair manner. We believe that S. 261 would have potentially unintended and inequitable consequences. We welcome the opportunity to work with the Committee to address our concerns.

Again, I thank you for the opportunity to be here, and I am happy to answer any questions that you may have.

In: The Federal Employees' Compensation Act ISBN: 978-1-62081-729-2
Editors: A. K. James and F. E. Davis

Chapter 5

STATEMENT OF GARY STEINBERG. HEARING ON "EXAMINING THE FEDERAL WORKERS' COMPENSATION PROGRAM FOR INJURED EMPLOYEES"*

Chairman Daniel Akaka, Ranking Member Ron Johnson, and members of the Subcommittee:

My name is Gary Steinberg, and I am the Acting Director of the Department of Labor's (DOL) Office of Workers' Compensation Programs (OWCP). OWCP administers a number of workers' compensation programs, including the Federal Employees' Compensation Act (FECA), which covers 2.7 million federal and postal workers and is one of the largest self-insured workers' compensation systems in the world.

I appreciate the opportunity to discuss legislative reforms to FECA that would enhance our ability to assist FECA beneficiaries to return to work, provide a more equitable array of FECA benefits, and generally modernize the program and update the statute. Almost 95 years ago, on September 7, 1916, Congress enacted FECA to provide comprehensive federal workers' compensation coverage to all federal employees and their survivors for disability or death due to an employment injury or illness. FECA's fundamental purpose is to provide compensation for wage loss and medical care, facilitate return to work for employees who have recovered from their injuries, and pay benefits to survivors. The faces of FECA include the postal

* This is an edited, reformatted and augmented version of the remarks given on July 26, 2011 before the Senate Committee on Homeland Security and Governmental Affairs.

worker whose mail truck is hit while delivering mail, the Federal Bureau of Investigation (FBI) agent injured or killed in the line of duty, the Department of Veterans' Affairs nurse who hurts her back while lifting patients, and the federal employee injured in the recovery efforts in Japan. All of these employees will receive benefits provided by this Act.

Since FECA has not been significantly amended in over 35 years, there are areas where the statute could be improved. Thus we have developed a number of proposals to reform and maintain FECA as the model workers' compensation program for the twenty-first century. In the 2012 Budget we estimated 10-year savings of around $400 million, but we think the potential savings are likely higher. After briefly discussing the current status of the FECA program, I am pleased to outline possible changes to the statute for consideration.

Many of the proposals are based on the results of studies by the program, the Government Accountability Office (GAO), the Inspectors General, as well as discussions with stakeholder organizations over the past 20 years. Recently, we have shared these proposed changes with staff of this and other Congressional committees and various outside parties such as representatives of federalemployee unions and members of the disability community.

FECA Today

Benefits under the FECA are payable for both traumatic injuries (injuries sustained during the course of a single work shift) and occupational disease due to sustained injurious exposure in the workplace. If OWCP's review of the evidence determines that a covered employee has sustained a work-related medical condition, the FECA program provides a wide variety of benefits including payment for all reasonable and necessary medical treatment; compensation to the injured worker to replace partial or total lost wages (paid at two-thirds of the employees' salary or at three-fourths if there is at least one dependent); a monetary award in cases of permanent impairment of limbs or other parts of the body; medical and vocational rehabilitation assistance in returning to work as necessary; and benefits to survivors in the event of a work related death.

FECA benefits are based upon an employee's inability to earn pre-injury wages with no time limit on wage loss benefit duration as long as the work-related condition or disability continues; the amount of compensation is based upon the employee's salary up to a maximum of GS-15 Step 10. More than

70% of FECA claimants are paid at the augmented (three-fourths) level. As workers' compensation benefits, they are tax free; long-term benefits are escalated for inflation after the first year of receipt.

FECA is a non adversarial system administered by OWCP. While employing agencies play a significant role in providing information to OWCP and assisting their employees in returning to work, the adjudication of FECA claims is exclusively within the discretion given to the Secretary of Labor by statute and is statutorily exempt from court review. Claimants are provided avenues of review within OWCP through reconsideration and hearing as well as an appellate forum, the Employees' Compensation Appeals Board (ECAB), a quasi-judicial appellate board within the DOL, completely independent of OWCP. FECA benefits are paid out of the Employees' Compensation Fund and most are charged back to the employee's agency. During the 2010 chargeback year, which ended on June 30, 2010, the fund paid more than $1.88 billion in wage-loss compensation, impairment, and death benefits and another $898.1 million to cover medical and rehabilitation services and supplies. These totals include outlays for non-chargeable costs for war risk hazards that total $86.2 million, primarily for overseas federal contractor coverage under the War Hazards Compensation Act (WHCA). Benefits paid have remained relatively stable at these levels for the past 10 years, with the exception of war risk hazard payments. In addition, the administrative costs to manage the program have consistently averaged a very modest 5% of total outlays. Although the program is almost 95 years old, OWCP's administration of FECA is by no means antiquated. All new claims are electronically imaged into a sophisticated paperless claims management system. Video and teleconferencing options are available to claimants to expedite the OWCP appeals process. Electronic Data Interchange capabilities are utilized by many of the program's agency partners. A secure, web-based electronic document-filing portal is currently under development; this new access will be deployed later this year and for the first time will be available to all system stakeholders, including injured workers and their physicians. This new tool will further reduce reliance on paper documents and shrink data input and imaging costs while speeding claim processing and reducing administrative costs.

Maintaining Program Integrity

OWCP actively manages the FECA program so that benefits are properly paid. After a case is accepted as covered, OWCP monitors medical treatment for consistency with the accepted condition -- if more than a very brief disability is involved, OWCP often assigns a nurse as part of our early nurse intervention program to assist with the worker's recovery and facilitate the return-to-work effort.

If disability is long-term, but the claimant can work in some capacity, a vocational rehabilitation counselor may be assigned to the case. Once a claim is accepted for ongoing, periodic payments, injured workers are required to submit medical evidence to substantiate continued disability (either annually or on a two or three year schedule for those less likely to regain the ability to work). Injured workers must cooperate with OWCP-directed medical examinations and vocational rehabilitation, accept suitable employment if offered and annually report earnings and employment (including volunteer work) as well as the status of their dependents and any other government benefits. OWCP claims staff carefully review these submissions and can require claimants to be examined by outside medical physicians to resolve questions on the extent of disability or appropriateness of medical treatment such as surgery.

OWCP also conducts monthly computer matches with the Social Security Administration (SSA) to identify FECA claimants who have died so that payments can be terminated to avoid overpayments. In addition, OWCP has conducted program evaluation studies to identify areas for process and policy improvements.

I noted earlier some of our case processing improvements. Based on the resulting recommendations and our claims experience, we have also improved how the program approaches disability management and return to work.

The program's early nurse intervention and quality case management initiatives are particularly noteworthy as the program evolves to reflect a renewed focus on return to work We have partnered with the Occupational Safety and Health Administration (OSHA) and our federal agencies to improve timely filing of claims and reduce lost production days.

As result of these efforts, the average number of days lost as a result of the most serious injuries each year has declined from 195 days in 1996 to 156 in 2010.

By speeding the average time to return to work in these cases, OWCP saves the government millions of dollars just in the first year of the injury; this also helps to avoid long term disability that can last for years thereafter.

A History of Performance

Under most circumstances FECA claims are submitted by employees to their employing agency, which completes the agency information required on the form and forwards the claim to OWCP. Over the past 5 years, an average of 133,000 new injury and illness claims were filed annually and processed by OWCP. The acceptance rate for new injury claims was 85%. Eighty-four percent (84%) were submitted within program timeliness standards of 10 working days and approximately 95% were processed by OWCP within program timeliness standards which vary depending on the complexity of the injury. Fewer than 15,000 of the accepted claims per year involve a significant period of disability. Eighty-five percent (85%) of claimants return to work within the first year of injury and a total of 89% return to work by the end of the second year. Due in part to OWCP's efforts to return injured employees to work, less than 2% of all new injury cases remain on the long-term compensation rolls two years after the date of injury. Currently, approximately 45,000 injured workers have long term ongoing disability benefits for partial or total wage loss, which they receive every 4 weeks. Some 15,000 are 66 years of age or older. (It should be noted however, that of this 15,000, over 7,000 have been determined to have no return-to-work potential, largely because of the substantial nature of their disability.)

FECA Reform

As I have discussed, OWCP has made significant administrative and technical changes to improve the administration of FECA. These changes were legally permissible within the existing statutory framework and had a demonstrable effect in advancing our progress. The current FECA reform proposal embodies certain reforms that can *only* be gained through statutory amendment that transforms FECA into a model twenty-first century workers' compensation program, increasing equity and efficiency while reducing costs. These amendments fall within three categories:

- Return to Work and Rehabilitation
- Updating Benefit Structures
- Modernizing and Improving FEC

Return to Work and Rehabilitation

The proposal that we have crafted for consideration would provide OWCP with enhanced opportunities to facilitate rehabilitation and return-to-work while simultaneously addressing several disincentives that may impact timely return to work by applying a new set of benefit rates prospectively to new injuries and new claims for disability occurring after enactment of the FECA amendments.

We propose additional statutory tools that would enhance OWCP's ability to return injured workers to productive employment. While FECA currently has the authority to provide vocational rehabilitation services and to direct permanently injured employees to participate in vocational rehabilitation, we suggest removing the permanency limitation in the statute to make clear that such services are available to all injured workers and that participation in such an effort is required. It is generally accepted and consistent with our experience that the earlier the claimant is involved in a vocational rehabilitation and a Return-to-Work program, the greater likelihood of a successful and sustained return to work post injury.

The proposal would amend FECA to explicitly allow for vocational rehabilitation, where appropriate, as early as six months after injury. It provides OWCP the authority to require injured claimants unable to return to work within six months of their injury to participate with OWCP in creating a Return–to-Work Plan where appropriate. The Return-to-Work Plan would generally be implemented within a two-year period. This provision would send a strong signal to all federal workers, whether injured or not, that the federalgovernment as a model employer is committed to doing everything it can to return employees to work as early as possible.

Our proposal would also amend FECA to provide permanent authority for what we call Assisted Reemployment. Assisted Reemployment is a subsidy designed to encourage employers to choose qualified rehabilitated workers whom they might otherwise not hire. As disabled federal workers with skills transferable to jobs within the general labor market may prove difficult to place due to economic factors, Assisted Reemployment is designed to increase the number of disabled employees who successfully return to the labor force by providing wage reimbursement to potential employers. Recent DOL appropriations bills gave OWCP the authority to provide up to three years of salary reimbursement to private employers who provide suitable employment for injured federal workers. Our data from our currently limited private sector program show that when we enter into an Assisted Reemployment agreement with a private employer, the employee is permanently hired by that employer at or beyond the 3 year period over 55% of the time. Of the employees not working for the same employer, approximately half are working with other employers. Because most federalemployees desire continued employment with the federal government, our proposal to expand this program to the federal sector would significantly increase its appeal and effectiveness. We are working closely with OPM and our partner agencies to actively seek re-employment opportunities for federal workers who become disabled as a result of work related injuries or illnesses. These provisions would assist with that effort and comport with and support the President's Executive Order 13548 to increase hiring of individuals with disability in the federal government. Under this proposal, OWCP would reimburse in part the salaries paid by federal agencies that hire workers with work-related injuries.

Return to work following an injury is often a difficult, painful process, requiring physical, mental and emotional adjustments and accommodations. If a workers' compensation system contains disincentives to return to work, that difficult transition back to work will occur more slowly, or in some cases, not at all. Where the medical evidence of ability to work is ambiguous and returning to work would require an employee to overcome actual physical limitations, these disincentives will exact a high price. That high price means a more costly program, lost productivity to the employing agency, and, for the workers themselves, disrupted lives and diminished self-esteem.

As currently structured, FECA creates direct disincentives to return-to-work in two significant ways. The first and most far-reaching is that while the basic rate of FECA compensation, 66 2/3%, is comparable to most state systems, many federal employees receive an augmented benefit, 75%, if they have at least one dependent. Computed at 75% tax free, FECA benefits often exceed the employee's pre-injury take home pay. Few state systems provide any augmentation for dependents, and none approaches the federal level.

Since the 75% compensation rate can result in benefits greater than the injured worker's usual take home pay, we also suggest amending FECA to provide that all claimants receive compensation at one uniform level of 70%. This compensation adjustment would remove disincentive to return to work, respond to equity concerns, and significantly simplify administration by greatly reducing documentation requirements for claimants and eliminating potential overpayments that can occur due to changes in dependency status. At this level compensation would remain quite adequate. A similar rate reduction is also proposed in death claims.

A second significant disincentive to return to work is created by the disparity that exists between the level of retirement benefits, provided by the OPM, received by most federal employees and the level of long-term FECA benefits for retirement age FECA recipients. Under current law, the thousands of long-term FECA beneficiaries who are over normal retirement age have a choice between federal retirement system benefits and FECA benefits, but they overwhelmingly elect the latter because FECA benefits are typically far more generous. OPM informs us that the average federal employee retiring optionally on an immediate annuity under the Civil Service Retirement System will receive about 60% of their "high-three" average salary, most of which is taxable, compared to a tax free 75% or 66.66% FECA benefit. The newer Federal Employees' Retirement System is designed to provide a comparable level of retirement replacement income from the three parts of its structure. Because returning to work could mean giving up a FECA benefit in favor of a lower OPM pension amount at eventual retirement, injured workers may have an incentive to consciously or unconsciously resist rehabilitation and instead, in certain cases, may cling to the self-perception of being "permanently disabled." In any event, the considerable difference between FECA benefits and OPM retirement benefits results in certain FECA claimants receiving far more compensation in their post retirement years than if they had completed their federalcareers and received normal retirement benefits like their colleagues. This disparity also suggests that a statutory remedy is needed.

This proposal provides claimants with a "Conversion Entitlement Benefit" upon reaching regular Social Security retirement age (and after receiving full benefits for at least one year) that would reduce their wage-loss benefits to 50% of their gross salary at date of injury (with cost of living adjustments), but would still be tax free. This benefit more closely parallels a regular retirement benefit, as opposed to a full wage-loss benefit, so that FECA recipients are not overly advantaged in their retirement years compared to their non-injured counterparts on OPM retirement. An injured worker receiving this retirement level conversion benefit would no longer be subject to several of the sanction provisions outlined in the FECA, such as forfeiture for failure to report earnings or the requirement to seek/accept suitable employment or participate in vocational rehabilitation. Even at this reduced rate, however, an injured worker would still be required to substantiate continuing injury-related disability or face suspension of compensation benefits.

UPDATING BENEFIT STRUCTURES

We also propose a number of changes to the current FECA benefit structure. One relates to the schedule award provision, which is designed to address the impact of impairment on an individual's life function, such as the loss of vision, hearing, or a limb. Impairment is permanent, assessed when an individual reaches maximum medical improvement, and is based upon medical evidence that demonstrates a percentage of loss of the affected member. Each member, extremity or function is assigned a specific number of weeks of compensation and the employee's salary is used to compute his or her entitlement to a schedule award. This payment structure results in considerable disparities in compensation: for example, a manager is paid far more than a letter carrier for loss of a leg even though the impact on the letter carrier may in reality be far more severe. In that instance, a GS-15 would receive twice what a GS-7 receives for the same loss of ability to get around, engage in recreational activities, etc., for this permanent impairment. Paying all schedule awards at the rate of 70% of $53,630 (the equivalent of the annual base salary of a GS 11 step 3) adjusted annually for inflation would certainly be more equitable.

Similarly, allowing injured workers to receive FECA schedule award benefits in a lump sum concurrently with FECA wage loss benefits for total or partial disability would provide a more equitable benefits structure for claimants. The current process is complicated and convoluted, often leaving injured workers frustrated and confused. It also can generate substantial unnecessary administrative burdens, as schedule award payments cannot be paid concurrently with FECA wage-loss benefits. To avoid the concurrent receipt prohibition some eligible claimants may elect OPM disability or retirement benefits, which they are allowed to receive for the duration of a schedule award. When the schedule award expires, they may elect to return to the more advantageous FECA wage-loss benefits. While they are collecting OPM benefits, OWCP and employing agency efforts to assist the employee in returning to work are stymied. In addition to switching to OPM benefits during the period of a schedule award, claimants can also switch back and forth between benefit programs over the life of a claim. As a result of these overly complex provisions and benefit streams, claimants sometimes do not return to work as early or as often as they could. By allowing concurrent receipt of these benefits, the claimant is timely compensated for the loss to the scheduled member and switching back and forth between OPM and OWCP benefits for this reason is eliminated. This allows a return-to-work or vocational rehabilitation effort to continue uninterrupted, thereby improving the chances of a successful return to employment. Finally, this proposal increases benefit levels for funeral expenses and facial disfigurement, both of which have not been significantly updated since 1949, to bring FECA in line with increases in other workers' compensation statutes.

MODERNIZING AND IMPROVING FECA

Because FECA has not been amended in over 35 years, updates are needed to modernize and improve several provisions of the statute. One such change was made several years ago but only applied to workers employed by the U. S. Postal Service (USPS). In order to discourage the filing of claims for minor injuries that resolve very quickly, state workers' compensation programs generally impose a waiting period before an injured worker is entitled to wage-loss compensation. Because of the way in which the 1974 amendments to FECA adding the "Continuation of Pay" provisions were drafted, the waiting period under FECA for traumatic injuries was effectively moved after the worker has received 45 days of "Continuation of Pay," thus defeating the purpose of a waiting period. The Postal Enhancement and Accountability Act of 2006 amended the waiting period for postal employees by placing the three-day waiting period immediately after an employment injury; we suggest placing the three-day waiting period immediately after an employment injury for *all* covered employees.

Another longstanding concern addressed by the proposal relates to the application of FECA subrogation provisions to claims. Workers' compensation systems generally provide that when a work-related injury is caused by a negligent third party the worker who seeks damages from that third party must make an appropriate refund to the workers' compensation system. As a result of the way in which the 1974 "Continuation of Pay" provision was drafted, OWCP cannot include amounts paid for Continuation of Pay in calculating the total refund to OWCP when a recovery is received by a FECA beneficiary from a third party.

OWCP also seeks the authority to match Social Security wage data with FECA files. While the SSA collects employment and wage information for workers, OWCP presently does not have authority to match that data to identify individuals who may be working while drawing FECA benefits. OWCP currently is required to ask each individual recipient to sign a voluntary release to obtain such wage information. Direct authority would allow automated screening to ensure that claimants are not receiving salary, pay, or remuneration prohibited by the statute or receiving an inappropriately high level of benefits. This proposal would also increase the incentive for employing agencies to reduce their injury and lost time rates. Currently the USPS and other agencies not funded by appropriations must pay their "Fair Share" of OWCP administrative expenses, but agencies funded by appropriations are not required to do so. Amending FECA to allow for administrative expenses to be paid out of the Employees' Compensation Fund and included in the agency chargeback bill, would increase federal agencies' incentive to reduce injuries and more actively manage return to work when injuries do occur.

To improve access to medical care, we suggest a provision that would increase the authority and use of Physicians' Assistants or Nurse Practitioners. We suggest amending FECA to allow Physicians' Assistants and Nurse Practitioners to certify disability during the Continuation of Pay period so that case adjudication is not delayed and treatment can be provided more rapidly. The provision allowing Physicians' Assistants and Nurse Practitioners to certify disability during the Continuation of Pay period would also reduce the burden of disability certifications in war zone areas because access to a physician may be even more limited in these circumstances.

To further address injuries sustained in a designated zone of armed conflict, FECA should be amended to provide Continuation of Pay for wage loss up to 135 days for such injuries. This increase from the standard 45 days would allow additional flexibility for claims handling in these challenging areas and is an outgrowth of a cooperative effort with OPM, the Department of State and the Department of Defense to address the needs of deployed civilian employees.

CONCLUSION

This proposal provides a fair and reasonable resolution to the disincentives and inadequacies that have arisen within the current FECA statute. Since any FECA reform should be prospective only, it would apply to new injuries and new claims of disability after enactment. Injured workers currently in receipt of disability benefits would see no changes in their benefit level. *This will allow all federal employees and federal agencies to embrace and adopt a more pro-active and progressive attitude about return to work and disability employment, and avoid any unfair interruption of benefits.* Even with this prospective approach, the ten-year cost savings are estimated to be around $400 million, or potentially even higher.

We believe that our proposals, if adopted, would allow all federalemployees and federal agencies to embrace and adopt a more pro-active and progressive attitude about return to work and disability employment, and avoid any unfair interruption of existing benefit streams.

The FECA program is at a critical juncture. We have done our best to keep the program current and responsive to the changing world we live in through administrative, technological and procedural innovations and investments. Without these statutory reforms, OWCP's best efforts may yield some further gains. However, we cannot overcome the fundamental disincentives in the current law and achieve the breakthrough improvements that we know are possible within the FECA program which will allow FECA to maintain its status as a model of workers' compensation programs.

The federal workforce comprises dedicated, hard working women and men that are committed to serving the public. OWCP is fully committed to ensuring that all injured workers receive the medical care and compensation they deserve, as well as the assistance needed to return to work when able to do so. FECA reform will enable OWCP to achieve those goals more effectively.

Mr. Chairman, I would be pleased to answer any questions that you or the other members of the committee may have.

In: The Federal Employees' Compensation Act ISBN: 978-1-62081-729-2
Editors: A. K. James and F. E. Davis

Chapter 6

FEDERAL WORKERS' COMPENSATION: QUESTIONS TO CONSIDER IN CHANGING BENEFITS FOR OLDER BENEFICIARIES*

United States Government Accountability Office

Chairman Akaka, Ranking Member Johnson and members of the Subcommittee:

I am pleased to be here today to comment on issues related to possible changes to the Federal Employees' Compensation Act (FECA) program, a topic that we have reported on in the past. At the end of chargeback year 2010, the FECA program, administered by the Department of Labor (Labor) had paid more than $1.88 billion in wage-loss compensation, impairment, and death benefits, and another $898.1 million for medical and rehabilitation services and supplies.[1] Currently, FECA benefits are paid to federal employees who are unable to work because of injuries sustained while performing their federal duties, including those who are at or older than retirement age. Concerns have been raised that federal employees on FECA receive benefits that could be more generous than under the traditional federal retirement system and that the program may have unintended incentives for beneficiaries to remain on the FECA program beyond the traditional retirement age. Over the past 30 years, there have been various proposals to change the FECA

---

* This is an edited, reformatted and augmented version of the GAO-11-854T Federal Workers Compensation, dated July 26, 2011.

program to address this concern. Recent policy proposals to change the way FECA is administered for older beneficiaries share characteristics with past proposals we have discussed in prior work. In August 1996, we reported on the issues associated with changing FECA benefits for older beneficiaries.[2] Because FECA's benefit structure has not been significantly amended in more than 35 years, the policy questions raised in our 1996 report are still relevant and important today.

My statement today will focus on (1) previous proposals for changing FECA benefits for older beneficiaries and (2) questions and associated issues that merit consideration in crafting legislation to change benefits for older beneficiaries. This statement is drawn primarily from our 1996 report in which we solicited views from selected federal agencies and employee groups to identify questions and associated issues with crafting benefit changes. For that report, we also reviewed relevant laws and analyzed previous studies and legislative proposals that would have changed benefits for older FECA beneficiaries. For purposes of this testimony, we did not conduct a legal analysis to update the results of our prior work, but instead relied upon secondary sources such as the Congressional Research Service (CRS). The work on which this testimony was based was conducted in accordance with generally accepted government auditing standards. Those standards require that we plan and perform the audit to obtain sufficient, appropriate evidence to provide a reasonable basis for our findings and conclusions based on our audit objectives. We believe that the evidence obtained provides a reasonable basis for our findings and conclusions based on our audit objectives.

In summary, we have reported that the perception that many retirement-age beneficiaries were receiving more generous benefits on FECA had generated two alternative proposals to change benefits once beneficiaries reach the age at which retirement typically occurs: (1) converting FECA benefits to retirement benefits and, (2) changing FECA wage-loss benefits by establishing a new FECA annuity. We also discussed a number of issues to be considered in crafting legislation to change benefits for older beneficiaries. Going forward, Congress may wish to consider the following questions in assessing current proposals for change: (1) How would benefits be computed? (2) Which beneficiaries would be affected? (3) What criteria, such as age or retirement eligibility, would initiate changed benefits? (4) How would other benefits, such as FECA medical and survivor benefits, be treated and administered? (5) How would benefits, particularly retirement benefits, be funded?

BACKGROUND

FECA

FECA is administered by Labor's Office of Workers' Compensation Programs (OWCP) and currently covers more than 2.7 million civilian federal employees from more than 70 different agencies. FECA benefits are paid to federal employees who are unable to work because of injuries sustained while performing their federal duties. Under FECA, workers' compensation benefits are authorized for employees who suffer temporary or permanent disabilities resulting from work-related injuries or diseases. FECA benefits include payments for (1) loss of wages when employees cannot work because of work-related disabilities due to traumatic injuries or occupational diseases; (2) schedule awards for loss of, or loss of use of, a body part or function; (3) vocational rehabilitation; (4) death benefits for survivors; (5) burial allowances; and (6) medical care for injured workers. Wage-loss benefits for eligible workers with temporary or permanent total disabilities are generally equal to either 66-2/3 percent of salary for a worker with no spouse or dependent, or 75 percent of salary for a worker with a spouse or dependent. Wage-loss benefits can be reduced based on employees' wage-earning capacities when they are capable of working again. OWCP provides wage-loss compensation until claimants can return to work in either their original positions or other suitable positions that meet medical work restrictions.[3] Each year, most federal agencies reimburse OWCP for wage-loss compensation payments made to their employees from their annual appropriations. If claimants return to work but do not receive wages equal to that of their prior positions—such as claimants who return to work part-time—FECA benefits cover the difference between their current and previous salaries.[4] Currently, there are no time or age limits placed on the receipt of FECA benefits.

With the passage of the Federal Employees' Compensation Act of 1916, members of Congress raised concerns about levels of benefits and potential costs of establishing a program for injured federal employees.[5] As Congress debated the Act's provisions in 1916 and again in 1923, some congressional members were concerned that a broad interpretation threatened to make the workers' compensation program, in effect, a general pension. The 1916 Act granted benefits to federal workers for work-related injuries. These benefits were not necessarily granted for a lifetime; they could be suspended or terminated under certain conditions. Nevertheless, the Act placed no age or time limitations on injured workers' receipt of wage compensation. The Act did contain a provision allowing benefits to be reduced for older beneficiaries. The provision stated that compensation benefits could be adjusted when the wage-earning capacity of the disabled employee would probably have decreased on account of old age, irrespective of the injury.

While the 1916 Act did not specify the age at which compensation benefits could be reduced, the 1949 FECA amendments established 70 as the age at which a review could occur to determine if a reduction were warranted.[6] In 1974, Congress again eliminated the age provision.[7]

Federal Retirement Systems

Typically, federal workers participate in one of two retirement systems which are administered by the Office of Personnel Management (OPM): the Civil Service Retirement System (CSRS), or the Federal Employees' Retirement System (FERS). Most civilian federal employees who were hired before 1984 are covered by CSRS. Under CSRS, employees generally do not pay Social Security taxes or earn Social Security benefits. Federal employees first hired in 1984 or later are covered by FERS. All federal employees who are enrolled in FERS pay Social Security taxes and earn Social Security benefits. Federal employees enrolled in either CSRS or FERS also may contribute to the Thrift Savings Plan (TSP); however, only employees enrolled in FERS are eligible for employer matching contributions to the TSP.

Under both CSRS and FERS, the date of an employee's eligibility to retire with an annuity depends on his or her age and years of service. The amount of the retirement annuity is determined by three factors: the number of years of service, the accrual rate at which benefits are earned for each year of service, and the salary base to which the accrual rate is applied.[8] In both CSRS and FERS, the salary base is the average of the highest three consecutive years of basic pay. This is often called "high-3" pay.

According to CRS, an injured employee cannot contribute to Social Security or to the TSP while receiving workers' compensation because Social Security taxes and TSP contributions must be paid from earnings, and workers' compensation payments are not classified as earnings under either the Social Security Act or the Internal Revenue Code. As a result, the employee's future retirement income from Social Security and the TSP may be reduced. Legislation passed in 2003 increased the FERS basic annuity from 1 percent of the individual's high-3 average pay to 2 percent of high-3 average pay while an individual receives workers' compensation, which would help replace income that may have been lost from lower Social Security benefits and reduced income from TSP.[9]

PROPOSALS TO CHANGE BENEFITS FOR OLDER BENEFICIARIES

Concerns that beneficiaries remain in the FECA program past retirement age have led to several proposals to change the program. Under current rules, an age-eligible employee with 30 years of service covered by FERS could accrue pension benefits that are 30 percent of their high-3 average pay and under CSRS could accrue almost 60 percent of their high-3 average pay. Under both systems benefits can be taxed.[10] By contrast, FECA beneficiaries can receive up to 75 percent of their preinjury income, tax-free, if they have dependents and 66-2/3 percent without dependents. Because returning to work could mean giving up a FECA benefit for a reduced pension amount, concerns have been raised by some that the program may provide incentives for beneficiaries to continue on the program beyond retirement age.

In 1996, we reported on two alternative proposals to change FECA benefits once beneficiaries reach the age at which retirement typically occurs: (1) converting FECA benefits to retirement benefits, and (2) changing FECA wage-loss benefits to a newly established FECA annuity.

The first proposal would convert FECA benefits for workers who are injured or become ill to regular federal employee retirement benefits at retirement age. In 1981, the Reagan administration proposed comprehensive FECA reform, including a provision to convert FECA benefits to retirement benefits at age 65. The proposal included certain employee protections, one of which was calculating retirement benefits on the basis of the employee's pay at time of injury (with adjustments for regular federal pay increases). According to proponents, this change would improve agencies' operations because their discretionary budgets would be decreased by FECA costs, and, by reducing caseload, it would allow Labor to better manage new and existing cases for younger injured workers. For example, a bill recently introduced in Congress includes a similar provision, requiring FECA recipients to retire upon reaching retirement age as defined by the Social Security Act.[11]

The second proposal, based on proposals that several agencies developed in the early 1990s, would convert FECA wage-loss compensation benefits to a FECA annuity benefit. These agency proposals would have reduced FECA benefits by a set percentage two years after beneficiaries reached civil service retirement eligibility. Proponents of this alternative noted that changing to a FECA annuity would be simpler than converting FECA beneficiaries to the retirement system, would result in consistent benefits, and would allow benefits to remain tax-free. Proponents also argued that a FECA annuity would keep the changed benefit within the FECA program, thereby avoiding complexities associated with converting FECA benefits under CSRS and FERS. For example, converting to retirement benefits could be difficult for some employees who currently are not participating in a federal retirement plan. Also, funding future retirement benefits could be a problem if the FECA recipient has not been making retirement contributions. Labor recently suggested a change to the FECA program that would reduce wage-loss benefits for Social Security retirement-aged recipients to 50 percent of their gross salary at the date of injury, but would still be tax-free.[12] Labor's proposal would still keep the changed benefit within the FECA program.

In our 1996 report, however, we identified a number of issues with both alternative proposals. For example, some experts and other stakeholders we interviewed noted that age discrimination posed a possible legal challenge and that some provisions in the law would need to be addressed with new statutory language.[13] Others noted that benefit reductions would cause economic hardships for older beneficiaries. Some noted that without the protections of the workers' compensation program, injured employees who have few years of service or are ineligible for retirement might suffer large reductions in benefits. Moreover, opponents to change also viewed reduced benefits as breaking the workers' compensation promise. Another concern was that agencies' anticipation of reduced costs for workers' compensation could result in fewer incentives to manage claims or to develop safer working environments.

QUESTIONS AND ISSUES TO CONSIDER IF CRAFTING FECA CHANGES

We also discussed in our 1996 report a number of issues that merit consideration in crafting legislation to change benefits for older beneficiaries. Going forward, Congress may wish to consider the following questions as it assesses and considers current reform proposals: (1) How would benefits be computed? (2) Which beneficiaries would be affected? (3) What criteria, such as age or retirement eligibility, would initiate changed benefits? (4) How would other benefits, such as FECA medical and survivor benefits, be treated and administered? (5) How would benefits, particularly retirement benefits, be funded?

How Would Benefits Be Computed?

The retirement conversion alternative raises complex issues, arising in part from the fact that conversion could result in varying retirement benefits, depending on conversion provisions, retirement systems, and individual circumstances. A key issue is whether or not benefits would be adjusted. The unadjusted option would allow for retirement benefits as provided by current law. The adjusted option would typically ensure that time on the FECA rolls was treated as if the beneficiary had continued to work. This adjustment could (1) credit time on FECA for years of service or (2) increase the salary base (for example, increasing salary from the time of injury by either an index of wage increases or inflation, assigning the current pay of the position, or providing for merit increases and possible promotions missed due to the injury).

Determining the FECA annuity would require deciding what percentage of FECA benefits the annuity would represent. Under previous proposals benefits would be two-thirds of the previous FECA compensation benefits. Provisions to adjust calculations for certain categories of beneficiaries also have been proposed. Under previous proposals, partially disabled individuals receiving reduced compensation would receive the lesser of the FECA annuity or the current reduced benefit. FECA annuity computations could also be devised to achieve certain benchmarks. For example, the formula for a FECA annuity could be designed to approximate a taxable retirement annuity. One issue concerning a FECA annuity is whether it would be permanent once set, or whether it would be subject to adjustments based on continuing OWCP reviews of the beneficiary's workers' compensation claim.

Which Beneficiaries Would Be Affected?

Currently most federal employees are covered by FERS, but conversion proposals might have to consider differences between FERS and CSRS participants, and participants in any specialized retirement systems.[14] Other groups that might be uniquely affected include injured workers who are not eligible for federal retirement benefits, individuals eligible for retirement conversion benefits, but not vested; and individuals who are partially disabled FECA recipients but active federal employees. With regard to vesting, those who have insufficient years of service to be vested might be given credit for time on the FECA rolls until vested. There is also the question of whether changes will focus on current or future beneficiaries. Exempting current beneficiaries delays receipt of full savings from FECA cost reductions to the future. One option might be a transition period for current beneficiaries. For example, current beneficiaries could be given notice that their benefits would be changed after a certain number of years.

What Criteria Would Initiate Changed Benefits?

Past proposals have used either age or retirement eligibility as the primary criterion for changing benefits. If retirement eligibility is used, consideration must be given to establishing eligibility for those who might otherwise not become retirement eligible. This would be true for either the retirement conversion or the annuity option. At least for purposes of initiating the changed benefit, time on the FECA rolls might be treated as if it counted for service time toward retirement eligibility. Deciding on the criteria that would initiate change in benefits might require developing benchmarks. For example, if age were the criteria, it might be benchmarked against the average age of retirement for federal employees, or the average age of retirement for all employees. Another question is whether to use secondary criteria to delay changed benefits in certain cases. The amount of time one has received FECA benefits is one possible example of secondary criteria. Secondary criteria might prove important in cases where an older, injured worker may face retirement under the retirement conversion option even when recovery and return to work is almost assured.

How Would Other Benefits, Such as FECA Medical Benefits or Survivor Benefits, Be Treated and Administered?

In addition to changing FECA compensation benefits, consideration should be given to whether to change other FECA benefits, such as medical benefits or survivor benefits. For example, the 1981 Reagan administration proposal would have ended survivor benefits under FECA for those beneficiaries whose benefits were converted to the retirement system. Another issue to consider is who will administer benefits if program changes shift responsibilities—OPM administers retirement annuity benefits for federal employees, and Labor currently administers FECA benefits. Although it may be advantageous to consolidate case management in one agency, such as OPM, if the retirement conversion alternative were selected, the agency chosen to manage the case might have to develop an expertise that it does not currently possess. For example, OPM might have to develop expertise in medical fee schedules to control workers' compensation medical costs.

How Would Benefits, Particularly Retirement Benefits, be Funded?

For the retirement conversion alternative, another issue is the funding of any retirement benefit shortfall. Currently, agencies and individuals do not make retirement contributions if an individual receives FECA benefits; thus, if retirement benefits exceed those for which contributions have been made, retirement funding shortfalls would occur. Retirement fund shortfalls can be funded through payments made by agencies at the time of conversion or prior to conversion. First, lump-sum payment could be made by agencies at the time of the conversion. This option has been criticized because the start-up cost was considered too high. Second, shortfalls could be covered on a pay-as-you-go basis after conversion. In this approach, agencies might make annual payments to cover the shortfall resulting from the conversions. Third, agencies' and employees' contributions to the retirement fund could continue before conversion, preventing shortfalls at conversion. Proposals for the FECA annuity alternative typically keep funding under the current FECA chargeback system. This is an annual pay-as-you-go system with agencies paying for the previous year's FECA costs.

In total, these five questions provide a framework for considering proposals to change the program.

Concluding Remarks

In conclusion, FECA continues to play a vital role in providing compensation to federal employees who are unable to work because of injuries sustained while performing their duties. However, continued concerns that the program provides incentives for beneficiaries to remain on the program at, and beyond, retirement age have led to calls for the program to be reformed. Although FECA's basic structure has not been significantly amended for many years, there continues to be interest in reforming the program. Proposals to change benefits for older beneficiaries raise a number of important issues, with implications for both beneficiaries and federal agencies. These implications warrant careful attention to outcomes that could result from any changes.

Mr. Chairman, this concludes my prepared statement. I would be pleased to respond to any questions that you or other members of the committee may have at this time.

End Notes

[1] FECA benefits are paid out of the Employees' Compensation Fund and most are charged back to the employee's agency. Labor's chargeback year for FECA agency billing purposes ends June 30, 2010.

[2] GAO, *Federal Employees' Compensation Act: Issues Associated With Changing Benefits for Older Beneficiaries*, GGD-96-138BR (Washington, D.C.: Aug. 14, 1996).

[3] Employees eligible for FECA benefits could also be eligible for retirement disability benefits from the Office of Personnel Management or Social Security Disability Insurance benefits from the Social Security Administration. Depending on which benefits employees are entitled to, employees might have to make an election between them. In many cases in which individuals receive benefits from different programs simultaneously, one benefit would likely be offset against the other to some extent.

[4] The maximum monthly FECA compensation payment cannot exceed 75 percent of the basic monthly pay for a GS-15, step 10 employee ($129, 517 per year as of Jan. 2, 2011). In general, OWCP continues to pay claimants the difference between their current salary and the salary they were earning at the time of their injury for as long as this difference exists and their medical work restrictions remains the same. (FECA benefits are indexed to the cost of living.) OWCP would not continue to pay this difference for claimants who quit their job without good cause (for example, if they quit because they did not like their work hours).

[5] 39 Stat. 742.

[6] 63 Stat. 854.

[7] Pub. L. No. 93-416, § 8, 88 Stat. 1143. According to Senate Report 93-1081, the Committee on Labor and Public Welfare stated that (1) the provision requiring the review of compensation was an unnecessary burden on both the injured employees and the Secretary of Labor (who had the authority to conduct the review); (2) age 70 had no bearing on one's entitlement to benefits; and (3) such a provision was discriminatory. FECA currently does not include a provision to change benefits based on retirement age.

[8] Under CSRS, a worker with at least 30 years of service can retire at the age of 55; a worker with at least 20 years of service can retire at the age of 60; and a worker with 5 or more years of service can retire at the age of 62. The FERS minimum retirement age for an employee with 30 or more years of service is 55 for workers born before 1948. A worker who has reached the minimum retirement age and has completed at least 30 years of service can retire with an immediate, unreduced annuity. A worker with 20 or more years of service can retire with

an unreduced annuity at age 60, and a worker with at least 5 years of service can retire at age 62 with an unreduced annuity.

[9] Pub. L. No. 108-92, 117 Stat. 1160 (2003).

[10] The replacement rate for a federal worker who retires with 30 years of service under CSRS is 56.25 percent. FERS accrual rates are lower than the accrual rates under CSRS because employees under FERS pay Social Security payroll taxes and earn Social Security retirement benefits. Estimating replacement rates under FERS is complicated by the fact that income from two of its components—Social Security and the TSP—will vary depending on the individual's work history, contributions to the TSP, and the investment performance of his or her TSP account.

[11] Federal Employees' Compensation Reform Act of 2011, S. 261, 112th Cong. (2011).

[12] According to CRS, an injured employee cannot contribute to Social Security or to the TSP while receiving workers' compensation because Social Security taxes and TSP contributions must be paid from earnings, and workers' compensation payments are not classified as earnings under either the Social Security Act or the Internal Revenue Code.

[13] Some argued that changing benefits for older beneficiaries violates protections against age discrimination contained in federal law by forcing them into accepting retirement benefits or a reduced annuity at a certain age.

[14] One conversion decision concerns whether to exempt injured workers who are ineligible for federal retirement benefits. Ineligible workers include, for instance, those without 5 years of federal service under CSRS, those who have withdrawn retirement contributions, temporary workers, and state and local police covered under special FECA provisions.

In: The Federal Employees' Compensation Act ISBN: 978-1-62081-729-2
Editors: A. K. James and F. E. Davis

Chapter 7

STATEMENT OF SUSAN M. CARNEY. HEARING ON "REVIEWING WORKERS' COMPENSATION FOR FEDERAL EMPLOYEES"*

Mr. Chairman and members of the Subcommittee,

My name is Sue Carney, and I am the National Human Relations Director for the American Postal Workers Union, AFL-CIO. The American Postal Workers Union is the world's largest postal union, representing more than 220,000 postal employees in the clerk, maintenance, and motor vehicle divisions and in support services; 50, 000 of which are veterans. We are employed in approximately 32,000 sites throughout the country, providing a public service in every city, town and community in our nation.

Workplace injuries, illnesses and deaths negatively impact a significant number of postal employees so we appreciate the opportunity to share our views regarding the Federal Employees Compensation Act (FECA) and the Department of Labor's proposed Federal Injured Employees Re-employment Act (FIERA). We believe various aspects of FECA and FIERA, if adopted as written, are disparaging and will negatively affect public servants and their families.

Furthermore, we would like to add that during a DOL briefing, the unions were adamantly advised that our concerns and objections would not be considered. Seemingly DOL used the occasion to gauge our response, rather

---

* This is an edited, reformatted and augmented version of the remarks given on May 12, 2011 before the House Education and Workforce Committee.

than consider the validity of our concerns, consequently amending some of their 'marketing strategies' to make the proposal appear more equitable. Additionally, they claim their reform proposals will "produce potential cost savings of approximately $400 million over a 10-year period for the American taxpayer." To our understanding the Office has not shared how it derived this figure, nor produced documentation to support it. It's noteworthy to point out that not all of the costs related to workplace injuries are borne by taxpayers. Also significant, wage loss compensation and death benefit costs have remained stable since 2001; however war risk hazard payments and escalating costs for medical and rehabilitation services and supplies brought a combined $367.3 million increase to the program[1]. It's our understanding that this figure includes all OWCP directed medical exams.

The FECA represents a longstanding covenant that our government made with federal workers. Each side gave up something to make it equitable and fair to both parties. Its primary purpose is to shield injured federal employees and their families from loss while limiting the employers' liabilities. "*The employer relinquished the defenses enjoyed under the common law, but this loss was offset by a known level of liability for work-place injuries and deaths. The employee gave up the opportunity for large settlements provided under the common law, but receives the advantage of prompt payment of compensation and medical bills. These tradeoffs make the federal workers' compensation system fair and equitable to both parties. However, where either party does not receive the benefits of this covenant, the system becomes unacceptable. When FECA was amended in 1974, Congress stated it is essential that injured or disabled employees of all covered departments and agencies, including those of the United States Postal Service, be treated in a fair and equitable manner. The Federal Government should strive to attain the position of being a model employer*".[2]

As we begin, it is important to point out that postal and federal workers are injured on the job because of the circumstances they encounter in performing a public service. These employees are victims of traumatic injuries such as slips and falls, muscle tears and herniated disc injuries. They are victims of poor ergonomic working conditions, like those that cause repetitive stress disease, making it difficult to perform simple tasks that involve grasping, holding and reaching. They suffer motor vehicle accidents, sustain injuries caused by faulty equipment and are innocent victims of unforeseeable, heinous crimes. Workplace injuries and diseases change lives; in many cases forever. No one ever goes to work wanting it to be the day they are injured or the day they will not return home to their family.

Injured workers do not reap greater benefits, nor do they lack motivation to return to work when capable, *as some have wrongfully implied.* In addition to the physical, mental and emotional pain that workplace injuries bring, it is important to understand the losses compensationers presently suffer before we consider asking more of these workers. They do not earn annual or sick leave. They are not able to contribute to the Thrift Savings Plan nor can they receive matching funds; this, in and of itself, causes a substantial loss for injured federal workers.[3] Their compensation rate remains locked at their date of injury (or first disability) pay rate. These employees do not receive the 'employer pay increases' they would otherwise be entitled to had it not been for their injury; only a COLA based on the Consumer Price Index (CPI), which has averaged just 2.1% annually over the last decade. Their lost workdays erode their Family Medical Leave balance, and they are often separated because of their disabilities. If separated prior to achieving the retention of health benefits and life insurance, these benefits are lost. When placed in the OWCP's vocational rehabilitation program they can expect to have their wage loss compensation reduced whether they are successful in obtaining employment or not.[4] In our opinion, these Division of Federal Employees Compensation (DFEC) procedures motivate and enable employers to refuse or withdrawal medically suitable work in order to escape a large portion of their chargeback liabilities; leaving injured workers with a significantly reduced or eliminated source of income.

FECA is supposed to be a non-adversarial, yet many workers and their physicians would disagree. In addition to the losses that were previously presented, let me share just a few examples of the adversarial scrutiny they are often subjected to. Physicians are frustrated. OWCP requires an extraordinary amount of paperwork from them and pays poorly for medical services; just 5% over the Medicare fee schedule. It is not enough for treating physicians to give their expert-medical opinion, confirming that a condition is work-related based on their examinations, testing and findings; their medical narratives are often rejected by claims examiners who have no medical background stating the doctor's opinion is not good enough because the doctor failed to share his or her reasoning. Prescribed medical treatment is often delayed or denied. In recent testimony presented by OWCP, the Acting Director stated "overcoming actual physical limitations exact a high price", which "means a more costly program". Taken in context, he seemed to imply that the Program will forgo the expense of medical treatment if it won't clearly result in a return-to-work.

Additionally, claimants are subjected to second opinions, and independent medical examinations, rather than trusting the opinion of the claimant's treating physician who understands the extent of the disability and is responsible for prescribing medical treatment. All of this needlessly adds to the cost of the program. These factors have made it difficult for claimants to find and keep doctors. When claimants do find doctors that are willing to treat them, claimants have been barred from using them if they are located further than 25 miles away. To the contrary, the Office regularly finds it acceptable to send claimants more than 100 miles away for their directed exams. DFEC also refuses to adjudicate questionable job offers for suitability; rather a claimant is required to refuse a job offer and risk going without income while the program takes months to make a suitability determination. These factors, coupled with the Office's recent and sweeping Proposed Rulemaking changes[5] and portions of the FIERA, all bring additional favor to employing agencies; cause unnecessary harm, in some cases irreparable harm, to injured workers and their families and do little to promote the non-adversarial program FECA is intended to be. They should not be permitted to stand.

EXAMINING FIERA PROPOSALS

Vocational Rehabilitation

We agree measures should be taken to help all injured workers return to suitable employment when their treating physician states that they are physically capable; however, granting authority to place employees with temporary medical restrictions into OWCP's vocational rehabilitation program is an objectionable approach. It would serve as further disincentive to employers who believe workers with disabilities are crippling their production. Currently, only employees with permanent medical restrictions can be voc-rehabbed. It's been our experience that employers regularly refuse work to these employees because they can escape chargeback through OWCP's vocational rehabilitation program due to loss wage earning capacity determinations. Comparatively, employers are more compelled to return employees with temporary restrictions to employment because they cannot be voc-rehabbed. In addition, premature vocational rehabilitation could interfere with the employees' prescribed recovery process or force employees to exceed their physical capacities. Recently, a Jacksonville OWCP District Office rehab counselor required a worker, who was only capable of working four hours a day, to interview for fifty jobs by the end of the week.

Additionally, the Office has not disclosed the specifics of its new Return-To-Work Plan for employees who are physically unable to be voc-rehabbed, nor has it shared if the employee's treating physician will be partnered into the process. According to figures provided by OWCP, only a mere 2% of all new injury claims remain on the long-term compensation rolls for more than two years. This demonstrates there is little need to compound the Program with additional rehabilitation costs.

To accomplish the goal of returning injured workers more readily to employment, we recommend that OWCP be more prompt in authorizing all recommended medical treatment, including physical therapy and surgeries which are often denied or delayed for extended periods of time.

Assisted Reemployment Program

The APWU can appreciate the Office's efforts to subsidize federal employment opportunities where suitable work does not actually exist within the worker's own employing agency; however, we are gravely concerned that such efforts would result in a reduction of compensation benefits. Again, the problem lies within the Office's LWEC procedures. DFEC procedure permits a reduction to wage loss compensation based on actual earnings. This alone is not objectionable, but, when the subsidized employment ends and residual disabilities remain there is no mechanism to reinstate the compensation that was eliminated. Another DFEC procedure permits LWECs based on constructed positions. Essentially, this permits a reduction in compensation even when the worker is unsuccessful in procuring a position. How is this fair and equitable?

We recognize that federal work cannot be used as a basis for making LWEC determinations, but the reality is, DFEC has advised it will look to comparable private sector positions to LWEC these employees. The Office has offered its Private-Sector Assisted Reemployment Program as an indicator of potential success for its Federal Assisted Reemployment Program. Interestingly, the Office has not disclosed how many private-sector program candidates they successfully placed in the program, nor has it advised how many LWEC's were issued as a result of the program, but we do know, based on figures provided by OWCP, that 45% of the employees who secured private –sector subsidized employment were not hired at or beyond the 3 year agreement period; consequently leaving many injured workers and their families at a deficit.

We recommend employers be required to provide compelling evidence when they assert that do not have medically suitable work for partially recovered employees and prove that they have taken all mandated measures to make reasonable accommodations for their disabled workers, before these workers are sent looking for work with other employers. In our opinion, the 'Federal' Assisted Reemployment Program would only be favorable if changes were made to reinstate lost compensation when employment stops and if constructed LWECs were eliminated. These actions would aid in facilitating employer cooperation, they are conducive to the President's Executive Order 13548, and would compel employers to retain their injured employees. On the surface, this proposal with all of its employer incentives could appear to inspire employers to hire injured workers; however, when you examine the existing procedures it would trigger, failure to incorporate our recommended changes creates the potential to bring irreparable harm to workers.

Conversion to Reduced Benefits for Total and Partial Disability at Retirement Age

To put matters into proper perspective, we should point out that regulations and procedures are so stringent it is virtually impossible to 'milk' the system *as is often implied.* This is evidenced in OIG's recent Semiannual Report to Congress where only twenty-three convictions for medical provider and claimant fraud were reported.[6] Compensationers are required to provide medical documentation on a fairly regular basis to support their disabilities in order to remain on the OWCP rolls. Compensationers aren't permitted to self-certify so it is meaningless for anyone to assert that injured workers may have an incentive "to cling to the self-perception of being permanently disabled." Even if they had that perception, it wouldn't be enough to keep them on the rolls. Furthermore, compensationers are regularly subjected to OWCP directed second opinion and independent medical examinations. Additionally, there is the existing and unforgiving OWCP Vocational Rehabilitation Program, so we must presume that many of the long-term compensationers are permanently and totally disabled; otherwise regardless of age, they would have been placed in OWCP's Vocational Rehabilitation Program to seek alternate employment.

It is wrong to infer that OWCP is a lucrative retirement program marked by disincentives that preclude employees from returning-to-work, as some have stated. It is also misleading and inequitable to compare annuitants who are able to achieve a 30 year career and obtain a true high three to compensationers who stop earning creditable service when they are separated for disability[7]. Compensationers do not receive the same salary increases their uninjured coworkers do. As we previously mentioned, their compensation is locked at their date of injury pay rate. It is disingenuous to cite CSRS as comparable. The federal retirement system converted to FERS in 1983. Since that was 28 years ago, and since FIERA is supposed to be prospective, the greatest majority of workers will fall under FERS. In either case, compensationers are not able to TSP, and are ineligible to receive matching contributions. Compensationers cannot contribute to Social Security and cannot receive credit for substantial earnings. Unlike their uninjured coworkers who can work after retirement to supplement their income, totally disabled compensationers are incapable of performing any work. The loss injured workers sustain by comparison is monumental. To reduce their compensation to 50% at a pre-selected and arbitrary age on the basis that CSRS annuitants receive a slightly higher but taxable percentage than that which is being proposed, is unfounded. To assume any age a 'normal' retirement age would be unjust, age discriminatory and presumptive. To the contrary, the Bureau of Labor Statistics reports more senior employees are opting to work well into their golden years to stay active and because they cannot afford to retire.[8] Do we really want to penalize seniors with work-related medical restrictions because of their age?

We would be remiss in assuming that our senior compensationers would have retired had they not been injured. We have to presume, based on existing OWCP procedures, that these employees are incapable of working otherwise OWCP would be derelict in performing its duties. For those who have temporary medical restrictions, it's important that we recognize they may be capable of working in the future once OWCP approves all prescribed treatment and the employee is given appropriate recovery time consistent with the nature of their injury. It would be punitive to reduce their wage loss compensation based on age and the time spent on the rolls. Recovery for extensive injuries can often take longer than a year.

Several measures can be taken to make FECA more fair and equitable. Laws could be changed to allow TSP withholdings and matching contributions; or a retirement fund, comparable to TSP could be created for compensationers that would permit employee withholdings and mandate employer contributions. Compensationers could be afforded the option to elect retirement based on an estimation of what their high-three would have been had they been able to continue their federal career. As it currently stands, employing agencies are the only benefactor.

Augmentation

Currently workers with dependents receive 75% of their pay, while workers without dependents receive 66 2/3%. DOL originally offered its proposal to convert all compensationers to 70% on the premise that workers with dependents do not earn more than those without. They also state the change would ease entitlement calculations for its claims examiners. Although it is true that workers with dependents do not earn more, tax deductions for these workers are less. This creates a larger net check to better support their families; workers without dependents net less. As to DOL's newer argument that FECA benefits frequently exceed the employee's pre-injury tax-home pay; there is no equity in being locked in at a rate that does not allow your usual pay increases. Additionally, uninjured coworkers are able to recoup tax withholdings by filing annual tax returns to add to their income; compensationers cannot. It is a ridiculous notion that claims examiners are being challenged by wage loss calculations with the technology that is available. The installation of a computer program or the use of a calculator would resolve the nuisance without going to the extreme of reducing benefits of worker families. APWU is opposed to any change that would burden families, or penalize workers because they are married and /or have children.

Scheduled Awards

Our primary objection to this proposal is based upon the change in pay rate percentages. It is our opinion that claimants should continue to receive their benefits based on their dependent status (75% dependents, 66 2/3% no dependents) for reasons we offered under augmentation. Moreover, we object to the GS 11 Step 3 rate ($53, 639.00) being used to calculate the value of scheduled awards. Historically, the employee's actual pay rate, at time of injury or first disability, whichever is greater, has been used to calculate scheduled awards. Today, this change would result in an increase for some claimants but a decrease for others. In the future however, it is likely that the GS-11 Step 3 rate would be even less reflective of the actual pay rates for some workers. Coupled with the DOL's recent adoption of the AMA Guide Sixth Edition, which significantly reduces impairment ratings and in turn considerably reduces the value of scheduled awards, the utilization of the GS 11 Step 3 rate would be a double-blow to compensationers who suffer a permanent loss of use.

In order to be equitable and fair the APWU recommends that scheduled awards remain based on the employee's pay rate. We strongly urge the DOL to convert back to using the AMA Guide Fifth Edition, in order to facilitate a more accurate means to rate impairments. There are no regulations that require DOL to use the latest edition of the AMA. In fact, AMA Guides Task Force Member, Matthew Dake, reports the AMA Sixth Edition is a flawed process that produces flawed results.

Death Benefits

Our objection to this proposal is based upon the change in pay rate percentages. It is our opinion that survivors should continue to receive their benefits based on the historic compensatory rate of 75%. A reduction does little more than swipe income from the spouses and children of federal workers who died providing a public service to our country.

Definition of New Claim for Disability

APWU has strong objections to this proposal. This is a veiled attempt to corral all compensationers, even those with existing approved claims into the FIERA. Passage would gather individuals submitting short-lived disability claims caused by a need to recover from physical therapy, spinal injection, surgery or other intermittent medical treatment. It would net claimants that experience a spontaneous worsening of an already accepted medical condition, and would also capture claimants who have medically suitable job offers withdrawn by employers, as is happening within the Postal Service in cataclysmic proportion. This is perhaps the slyest of all the DOL proposals. The DOL leaves many with the impression that FIERA is prospective as it will only affect individuals with "new" claims, but in reality DOL is attempting to change the understood definition of what is "new". Passage of this proposal would afford employing agencies even greater favor by burdening a significantly greater number of injured workers and their families. All Compensation Act submissions require adjudication but traditionally only two are considered new claims. The definition of a new claim should remain limited to traumatic injuries and occupational disease.

Burial Expenses

This update is long overdue; however APWU would suggest the benefit be more reflective of actual final expenses. According to the National Funeral Directors Association, the average cost in 2009 was $7,755.00.

Computation of Pay

Workplace injuries are not supposed to cause loss to workers. Therefore, compensation is purposeful in including all of the pay factors that an employee would have been entitled to had they not been injured. Traditionally, compensation is based on an employee's salary, including night differential, Sunday premium pay and holiday pay, and for some workers includes overtime. Quite simply, APWU objects to compensation being paid at any rate other than the employee's actual pay rate at time of injury or first disability, inclusive of all usual entitlements to Sunday premium, night differential, holiday pay and where appropriate overtime pay. It should not be based or capped on an arbitrarily selected GS rating, which would create a pay increase for some employees and a decrease for others. It is neither fair nor equitable to generate savings for employers off the backs of injured workers. Furthermore, we will restate that it is a ridiculous notion that claims examiners are being challenged by wage loss calculations with the technology that is available.

Waiting Period

Continuation of Pay, its very spirit is stated in its name. It is in place to ensure employees and their families have an income while OWCP adjudicates their claim. Despite OWCP's testimony, it often takes 60 – 120 days for claims to be approved and for wage loss compensation to begin. The APWU is opposed to federal employees being subjected to a three-day waiting period. All workplace injuries are real; even minor ones. This fact does not make them frivolous. Employees are subjected to the same scrutiny and requirements for minor injuries. They still need to meet the same five requirements to achieve claim approval, one of which includes a medical narrative with medical reasoning. A three day waiting period has been unjustly imposed upon Postal Workers in order to save money for the employer. The same should not be imposed upon federal workers. APWU would request the three day waiting period be removed from COP for postal workers. This action would satisfy the stated goal of uniformity and enable COP to fulfill its intended purpose.

Sanction for Non-Cooperation with Nurses

To impose sanctions for non-cooperation with nurses means to eliminate eligibility for wage loss compensation and scheduled awards. The nurse intervention program is already fraught with overzealous nurses who attempt to impede or redirect the prescribed medical treatment of the claimant's treating physician, and who impose themselves in private examinations and doctor patient discussions. APWU is opposed to giving these nurses the authority to have sanctions initiated without first giving claimants access to due process.

Compensation for Foreign Nationals

Upgrades to this provision are long overdue. However, since these foreign nationals are performing a public service for our country, APWU believes they should be compensated using the same percentage ratings that apply to our claimants (75% dependents, 66 2/3% no dependents).

CONCLUSION

Although we are very disappointed with portions of FECA, many of the FIERA proposals, and some of the Office's action, we still believe the Department of Labor is the best means available to handle the claims process for all federal and postal workers. APWU feels strongly that the Federal Workers Compensation Program (OWCP DFEC) should continue to strive to be a model program, not work to be comparable to insufficient state programs. To help OWCP meet its burden, it is our opinion that more claims examiners are needed. To eliminate some of the erratic decisions claimants are receiving all claims examiners should be required to receive, on a regular basis, more comprehensive training regarding regulations, procedures and precedent setting Employees Compensation Appeals Board decisions.

We also believe efforts should be made to recreate the non-adversarial atmosphere that the Program is intended to be. To help accomplish this we recommend more substantive outreach to employee representatives and more meaningful technical assistance to treating physicians and claimants who are often confused by the processes. Efforts should be made to make the Program more palatable for doctors.

Many forgo treating claimants because of the extraordinary reporting requirements and low reimbursement rate for services. It is our opinion that OWCP should be granted moderate enforcement authority to compel employers, who have been skirting return-to-work obligations and other responsibilities to comply. We would also implore the Committee to work to create more meaningful safety and health mandates to protect workers, and provide better mechanisms to enforce them. These initiatives alone could reduce the overall cost of workplace injuries and disease.

Bending policy and recreating procedures to favor agencies do little to maintain a fair and equitable atmosphere. Shrouding them as "modernization, return-to-work and administration simplification" is disingenuous. As we examine the history presented by the Congressional Research Service, we would request that we be mindful not to regress but rather progress. Before we consider passing legislative changes, we must ensure they are meaningful changes and examine how the consequences of our actions will impact workers and their families.

We thank you for your time and consideration regarding this paramount issue. I am available to answer any questions you may have to further clarify your understanding of the compensation processes and of our concerns.

End Notes

[1] War risk hazard payment $86.2 million(WHCA); increase cost for medical services $281.1 million

[2] Excerpt from Joseph Perez's statement when appearing before The House Government Reform and Oversight Committee Government Management, Information and Technology Subcommittee on July 6, 1998. Perez is a former OWCP DFEC Claims Examiner and currently practices law.

[3] The TSP Calculator illustrates that an employee who is earning $40,000 annually, contributing 10% and receiving the employer's maximum 5% contribution over the span of a 30 year career, and who is earning an average of 5% interest is estimated to realize more than$416,000 towards his / her retirement savings

[4] Division of Federal Employees Compensation Procedure Manual Part 2 Chapter 0814 Sections 7 and 8. These actions are known as loss wage earning capacity (LWEC) determinations. In basic terms, a LWEC is a comparison between wages of actual or potential earnings against wages at the time of injury. The difference is what the claimant is entitled to receive in wage loss compensation. For example, a worker was making $20 hr when injured. They normally would receive $15 in WLC if they have dependents, but if the Office finds a

potential job that pays $18 hourly, the employee is then only entitled to receive 75% of the difference, which in this scenario would be $1.50 hourly, even when the employee was an unsuccessful applicant. And if the employee procured the job but subsequently the job was withdrawn, the employee would still only be entitled to $1.50 per hour in WLC.

[5] RIN 1240-AA03

[6] April 1 – September 30, 2010

[7] Employers are permitted and generally do separate employees who are collecting wage loss compensation for one continuous year.

[8] The Bureau of Labor Statistics indicates that as of 2007, 56.3% of workers age 65 and older have opted for fulltime employment over part-time employment. That employment of workers ages 65 and over has increased 101 % between 1977 and 2007: men rose by 75%; women climbed by 147%; while workers 75 and over had the most dramatic gain, increasing by 172%. There is also an apparent failure to acknowledge that projected growth in the labor force for workers between the ages of 65 and 74 is predicted to soar by 83.4 percent between 2006 and 2016. The number of workers age 55-64 is expected to climb by 36.5 percent. By 2016, workers age 65 and over are expected nearly double its participation in the total labor force from that of 2006.

In: The Federal Employees' Compensation Act ISBN: 978-1-62081-729-2
Editors: A. K. James and F. E. Davis

Chapter 8

STATEMENT OF USPS INSPECTOR GENERAL DAVID C. WILLIAMS. HEARING ON "FECA: A FAIR APPROACH"*

Mr. Chairman and members of the subcommittee, thank you for the opportunity to discuss workers' compensation issues and reform. The Federal Employees Compensation Act (FECA) requires federal agencies to participate in the Department of Labor's (DOL) FECA program. DOL bills each agency annually for compensation paid and non-appropriated agencies also must pay DOL an annual administrative fee. Eligible disabled employees receive 66 2/3 percent (or 75 percent with dependents) of their basic salary, tax-free plus, medical-related expenses. Also, FECA places no age limit on receiving benefits. This is substantially more than other employees receive when they retire. Though unintended, FECA has become a lucrative retirement plan.

The Postal Service is the largest FECA participant, paying more than $1 billion in benefits and $60 million in administrative fees annually, creating a long-term liability of $12.6 billion. As of February 2011, the Postal Service had about 15,800 disabled employees. Over 8,700 were at least age 55, about 3,100 were at least age 65, and about 900 were between age 80 and 98.

Certain aspects of the program make it susceptible to fraud:

- The claimant's ability to change their story until their claim qualifies;
- The claimant's ability to hire a physician rather than use a plan physician to assess their injuries and condition;

* This is an edited, reformatted and augmented version of the remarks given on April 13, 2011 before the House Committee on Oversight and Government Reform.

- The program incentivizes DOL to collect larger fees if they approve more claims and lose budget dollars if they deny them;
- The lack of effective DOL case management; and
- Employers not being allowed to present or respond to evidence at hearings.

DOL has some fraud detection responsibility, but it's unclear to what extent. They advise agencies to actively manage their own programs, while still charging administrative fees. There is not a clear delineation of responsibility between **(1)** agency program managers and **(2)** their OIGs and **(3)** DOL and **(4)** its OIG in detecting fraud. Accordingly, there is significant risk that program oversight will be duplicative or not done.

Since October 2008, we have removed 476 claimants based on disability fraud, recovered $83.5 million in medical and disability judgments, and halted significant future losses. In one investigation, a fraudulent claimant received $142,000 in benefits while she was working as a real estate agent, and we had pictures of her hiking and bungee jumping. She even bought a boat named "Free Ride." Other investigations have found fraudulent claimants working as martial arts instructors, landscapers, hairdressers and mechanics.

Working with DOL is difficult. They control needed documents, but are often not responsive when we investigate cases. Additionally, they do not take timely action when told that a claimant no longer qualifies for benefits. Even when a claimant is convicted, DOL is slow to terminate benefits.

- We gave DOL an investigative report in 2006 which found a claimant was exceeding his limitations. Even though the employee was willing to return to work, DOL did not reduce his benefits until 2011.
- Fourteen months ago we gave DOL an investigative report containing evidence of fraud by a disability claimant and a subsequent medical exam confirmed the claimant was able to return to work with no restrictions. Despite requests, DOL has taken no action and continues to pay benefits.
- Over a 5-year period one claimant submitted $190,000 in unsupported mileage reimbursements that DOL paid without question.

Stress claims in particular are at high risk for fraud. If a doctor sees a correlation between stress and a claimant's work, the claim is often approved. In one instance, a claimant's emotional reaction to a change in work schedule was enough for DOL approval.

The OIG also investigates medical providers involved in criminal matters, including disability fraud and we have recovered $78.5 million since FY 2009. Unfortunately, DOL provides no standardized billing guidelines for doctors, making it difficult to hold them accountable for fraudulent billings. If DOL instituted a system similar to Medicare's, prosecutors would be more inclined to take these cases.

From our reviews, the Postal Service would benefit from having its own workers' compensation program. Savings would be in the areas of reduced administrative fees, accurate assessment of claims by plan physicians, buyout options, mandatory retirements, immediate access to records, and improved accountability over case management.

FECA is in need of significant reform. Such reform could reduce the substantial risk for fraud and improve program efficiency and effectiveness, while protecting reasonable benefits for legitimate claimants.

INDEX

D

E

F

G

H

I

T

U

V

W

Y